The Art of Making Vegetarian Sausages

Stanley Marianski, Adam Marianski

Bookmagic, LLC
Seminole, Florida

ISBN: 978-0-9904586-3-0
Library of Congress Control Number: 2015911013

Bookmagic, LLC.
www.bookmagic.com

Printed in the United States of America.

Contents

Introduction

For thousands of years the definition of sausage was meat stuffed into a casing. The composition of sausages started to change after the first and second world wars due to widespread famine, depletion of livestock and damaged cities. Hunger forced people to improvise - different filler materials found their way into sausages. Potatoes, rice, dry wheat rolls, buckwheat groats, barley, oats, bread crumbs, ground corn, soy beans and flours started to appear along with meat in a variety of sausages. There were, however, certain established rules for making meat sausages.

Vegetarians also started to incorporate sausages into their dishes but with few restrictions. Vegetarian sausage recipes which can be found on the internet are simply food dishes with a sausage being one of many components. This can extend to simply cutting up a store-bought vegan hot dog and serving it with rice on a plate. There are meat or vegetarian patties that somehow get to be called sausages. If a filler material, meat or non-meat, is not stuffed into a casing it is not a sausage. It is not enough to stuff tofu or other materials into a casing and call it it a sausage. A vegetarian sausage must look like a sausage, have the texture of a sausage and most importantly, it should taste good. It does not need to mimic the meat sausage's flavor and the time has arrived to place vegetarian sausages in their own category as a unique product.

Almost all commercially produced vegan sausages are emulsified, similar to hot dogs, as it is easy to emulsify all ingredients in a food processor and call it a sausage. They all look and taste alike, with flavor that is unremarkable. It is more challenging to make a large oblong shaped sausage with rice, raisins and nuts inside that can be sliced thinly and will not break apart. The choice of raw material in meat sausages is rather limited and usually includes pork, beef and spices. Too much innovation may not be accepted by a customer as meat sausages have been defined throughout history. On the other hand, making vegetarian sausages is a newly developing art with none of the rigid standards and established practices. Vegetarian sausage is a product in its own class that does not need to be compared with meat sausages at all. Vegetarian sausage should not be thought of as the poor cousin of a meat sausage. It can take its own place not only as a healthier option, but also as a highly diversified quality product.

Imagination is the limit and vegetarian sausages can be made with almost any ingredients. A good cook will likely be a good sausage maker. Look at candy snacks; they are made with peanut butter, almonds, coconut, and chocolate. They are creamy and crunchy, they are like little sweet sausages stuffed into a wrapping. Yet they hold their shape when the wrapping is removed. This is how vegetarian sausages should be made, they should hold their own when the casing is removed. Incorporating filler material into sausages was practiced throughout history. It was common in Europe after the end of World War II and has been practiced in poor countries in South America and Asia.

What in the past was looked down upon as being inferior by the well to do Westerners was actually a healthy sausage of the poor. They ate healthier food, being physically active they were also thinner and fit. Our attitude towards food has been recently changing and we are starting to accept and "love" food on which we have looked at with disdain in the past. The best example is a case of polenta which was once considered a peasant food and now is available in every supermarket. Nothing prevents us from introducing grains such as quinoa from Peru or teff from Ethiopia into vegetarian sausages.

Poor man's food is a healthy food.

Vegetarian sausages are starting to appear in supermarkets where shelf space is judged at the price of gold. They all look like hot dogs, they are all made with tofu, they are all brown and they all have a rather poor flavor. Vegetarian sausages deserve better than being just an imitation of a meat hot dog. They can be made from hundreds of different materials and be presented in many colors, something that cannot be done with meat which by its nature imparts a red color to the product. A hobbyist can experiment with different materials and create an infinite number of sausages, something that a commercial producer will never risk.

After making sausages all my life and writing 10 books on the subject, I have decided to challenge my skills and knowledge and discover the best methods for making vegetarian sausages at home. The project has been a challenging one as there was not any scientific information that can be used as a reference. It came as a shock to me that with millions of pages on the internet and thousands of universities and food organizations, there was very little information on the subject of making vegetarian sausages. Many experiments were conducted and some recipes were made many times over until the correct formula was discovered. Slowly, like a light in a tunnel, certain rules started to emerge and everything started to fall into place. The purpose of this book is to convince the reader that he can make sausages from any ingredient available. He will be able to create his own recipes and control the texture and color of his product while ending up with a delicious piece of food.

Stanley Marianski

6

Chapter 1

Vegetarian Sausages

Vegetarians

If someone refers to themselves as vegetarian, the general assumption is that they are lacto-ovo vegetarian. That means they don't eat animal products that require the killing of an animal, but eggs and dairy are fine. Rennet and gelatin are options they may or may not include. Some vegetarians will just simply not eat red meat, but will eat fish and poultry. A person who eats fish and/or poultry is by no means a vegetarian, just a selective omnivore. Gelatin comes from a dead animal, it is derived from pork skins, pork, horses, cattle bones, or split cattle hides so it is not a vegetarian ingredient.

Vegans

Vegans in the strictest sense will not eat any animal flesh, nor will they eat animal derived products. In the purest sense a strict vegan will exclude dairy and honey.

Vegetarian Sausages

Vegetarian sausages are much healthier as they don't contain animal fat or cholesterol. There is no need to worry much about factors like smoke temperature or freezing meat and fat before grinding, however, they do present more problems with the texture. The manufacturing process follows general sausage making steps, but is somewhat simpler as it does not involve curing or smoking. Most sausages can be made without using a grinder at all. In addition non-meat materials present less safety hazards than meat which is at risk of being infected with pathogenic bacteria. Raw materials such as flour or grains can be stored at room temperature, a procedure which cannot be applied to meat.

What is a Vegetarian Sausage?

Well by traditional definition a sausage was meat that was stuffed into a casing. When the first sausages were made we probably did not know how to grow crops or make products like tofu, so the sausages were made with meat. The manufacture of food products in the past was based not on the quality or flavor of the product, but by the necessity of the survival - if it lasted longer than a few days it was a good food. Does a bear worry about the flavor of the product he consumes? He worries about the amount of food he needs to store in order to survive the winter. As meat and especially fat rank on top of food products rich in calories, it is not surprising that eating berries, grains or other non-animal products was not the priority. A pound of fat supplies 4,077 calories which is enough to sustain body functions for 2 days. No other food is even close in caloric value so it is not surprising that meat and fat were held in such a high esteem. In time as we started to cultivate grains new products appeared such as bread and porridge. Grains like barley, buckwheat or rice were added to meat to extend its value. The choice of a filler material was not dictated by its flavor, but by its availability in a local area. The food shortages and famine, especially after the first and the second world wars contributed to the development of sausages which in addition to meat also contained fillers such as potatoes, dry rolls, bread crumbs, rice, potato and semolina flours, corn meal, and barley and buckwheat grains.

Most commercially produced vegetarian sausages are of emulsified type, eg. veggie hot dogs. It is much easier to place everything into a food processor and then stuff the resulting paste into a casing. They look like meat hot dogs, unfortunately they don't taste like them. Vegetarian sausages which *are not emulsified* in a food processor are harder to make. The difficulty lies in controlling texture, it is much harder to produce a vegetarian sausage that contains rice, barley or oats and to bind those materials with spices in such a way that they will not crumble when the sausage is thinly sliced. Unlike traditional home-made meat sausages, the casing is not made of animal intestine but of synthetic ingredients.

When the texture is under control, the sausage can contain an infinite number of materials, some of which may be considered "show" pieces. For example, slices of rehydrated apples or plums, raisins, olives or nuts. Filler materials such as tofu, potatoes, barley, rice, oats, rusk, bread crumbs and soaked bread can be used. Potato flakes, potato flour, chickpea flour, semolina, rice flour, starches and textured vegetable protein can be added as well. Most people love bread pudding and bread pudding sausage can easily be made. There is no shortage of ingredients and hundreds of recipes can be created.

The hardest problem to solve is to duplicate the flavor of meat. It would be advisable to accept the fact that a sausage that is made without meat has a different flavor and cannot compete with a traditionally made meat product. The faster you free your mind from the notion that a vegetarian sausage must mimic the flavor of the meat sausage the faster you will start making great vegetarian sausages. They don't need to imitate meat sausages, they can shine in their own limelight. There are thousands of sausage recipes on the Internet where an author chops a store bought sausage, serves it on a plate with rice and beans and calls it a sausage recipe. Well it might be called a new sausage recipe, but it has little to do with making sausages.

Texture in Meat Sausages

The main difficulty with making vegetarian sausages is the texture. As they do not contain meat protein or solid fat, new procedures must be introduced to bypass the established ways of making sausages. The following information is of crucial importance as it will enable you to understand how the texture in meat sausages is formed and what can be done to improve the texture of vegetarian sausages.

Meat sausages - the texture of meat sausages is influenced by the amount of meat glue (exudate) produced by meat proteins and the amount of gelatin obtained form collagen which resides in meat cuts rich in connective tissue. ***Proteins*** are released from muscles during cutting or grinding and then dissolve in salt and water creating a sticky liquid that *glues* meat particles together. Grind lean meat through a fine plate, add salt and start mixing or rather kneading the mass for 5 minutes. The mass becomes sticky because meat starts to release proteins which dissolve in salt producing a sticky substance. Sausage makers mix meat with spices until the meat *releases the glue* and then the sausage is stuffed.

Meat cuts rich in **connective tissue (collagen)** contribute to binding of meat particles, in other words to its texture. Sinews, gristle, silver screen, pork cheeks (jowls), feet, skins, generally speaking parts rich in connective tissue are emulsified and become a paste. These parts contain collagen which upon heating becomes a liquid *gel* which acts like a glue. The gel is reversible and upon cooling becomes a solid clear gel that holds particles together. Those parts are needed for making traditional head cheese, meat jelly, liver sausages or any quality meat product, however, a commercially produced gelatin which is made from pork skins will produce the same effect. Additionally, collagen is able to bind water which provides more juiciness to the product. There is no need for extra ingredients or chemicals as the meat contains all that is needed to produce a great product. Fresh meat, salt and pepper are all that is needed.

Fat - any sausage, whether made with meat or not needs some fat. The fat carries the flavor and provides a pleasant slippery sensation known as "mouthfeel" to our tongue. The undisputed fact remains that man has evolved as a carnivorous creature which can be attributed to many factors:

- a slaughtered animal satisfied the tribe's needs for many days.

- meat, especially fat, supplies plenty of calories. No vegetables, fruits or berries can match the calories provided by meat. For people living in cold climates those calories were needed not just to satisfy hunger, but also to maintain body temperature and that requires plenty of fuel. Most cold climate animals would not survive the winter if they did not accumulate a sufficient amount of fat in the summer.

- in northern areas the availability of fruits or berries were limited to just a few months of the year, but animals were always around.

- for most of his existence man did not know how to grow foods. The man was a hunter and not a farmer.

By eating meat, fish, birds and eggs our palate has grown accustomed to the sensation of fat which is not easy to duplicate. Only in recent years the latest discoveries have opened a path for making low fat products that have an acceptable taste and flavor. Anything containing fat provides a satisfying feeling-bacon, mayonnaise, cream cheese, chocolate, ice cream, butter, full milk-the list does not end.

Make coffee with non-fat milk and one with full milk and you will taste the difference. You cannot make top quality sauce without butter. We are not advocating choosing a high cholesterol diet, we are simply trying to establish basic facts as they relate to making quality sausages. A hamburger made from very lean meat tastes like a pile of bread crumbs, but the one with 25% fat is defined as juicy.

If you want to save on fat, you have to increase the moisture content what will make the sausage feeling juicer to our tongue. You can also use commercially prepared fat replacers, for example a combination of konjac gum, xantham gum and microcrystalline cellulose. When solid fat is heated it will melt but when subsequently cooled it solidifies again becoming solid. This also greatly contributes to a better texture of meat sausages.

Texture in Vegetarian Sausages

All grains and legumes contain some protein, however, soy beans produce powders with a protein count over 90%. Our discussion does not include protein made from milk or whey. Unlike meat proteins, vegetable proteins do not produce "glue" when cut in the presence of salt, however, they can bind some water. We could bind a lot of water with gums, but the resulting gel is soft like a fruit jelly and the sausage will be too soft to cut. To produce a firm sausage use as little water or moist ingredients as possible. Obtaining a good texture is harder to accomplish with veggie sausages because traditionally used binders such as egg white, gelatin, or non fat dry milk are not used by vegetarian purists. There is, however, a variety of ingredients which when smartly used will produce a sausage with a good texture. Flaxseed emulsion, described later, is quite sticky and contributes positively to a stronger texture.

Photo 1.1 White long rice, apple sauce and raisins perfectly bound together.

The sausage must look and feel like a sausage. When it is cut across, each slice should keep together and hold its own. The casing should peel off easily. Would you buy sliced ham or bologna that would break into many individual pieces?

Photo 1.2 The casing should peel off easily.

Once the sausage has been cut its texture will improve and the sausage will firm up due to evaporating moisture, even when kept in a refrigerator. The texture can be controlled with:

- Emulsions - soy protein or flaxseed.
- Hydrocolloids - gums made from seaweeds which are used by the food industry. Flours and starches may be considered simple gums.

Photo 1.3 Wild rice, celery, green peppers, red bell and jalapeno peppers perfectly bound together.

Fat. Insufficient amounts of fat and resulting poor mouthfeel in vegetarian sausages can be corrected by introducing vegetable oil. Oil like any fat drastically increases the calorie count in any product. To lower the amount of oil and still preserve a reasonably good mouthfeel more water must be added providing the proper steps are taken to permanently bind this water inside. This produces a stronger sensation of "juiciness" and better mouthfeel. The extra amount of water can be immobilized by starch or gums, but there is a danger of the sausage becoming too soft. The vegetable oil is liquid at room temperature, it is liquid when heated, and remains liquid when cooled. *It does not solidify.* If too much is added, the sausage will become soft and oily. So the application of oil can be a tricky one and to be on the safe side, a little goes a long way.

The best way to apply oil is to hide it inside emulsion. A good example is mayonnaise which is all oil, yet we do not see it. Mayonnaise is an egg emulsion, all that is needed is the yolk of an egg, oil and a whisk. In the photo below each emulsion contains 40% oil. The amount of oil could be increased, however, this might make the sausage too soft. Emulsions are covered in detail in Chapter 4.

Photo 1.4 Protein emulsions, from the left: soy, soy with beet juice, flaxseed, soy with annatto.

12

Flavor

The flavor of sausage is the sum of texture, flavor of basic materials, spices, the amount of fat and the amount of water. There is not one unique meat flavor, pork, beef, sheep, poultry and fish have different colors and flavor. Even different meat cuts from the same animal exhibit different flavors: pork belly, loin, shoulder or liver, they all have different flavor. Meat coming from older animals has a more pronounced flavor. Vegetarian sausages are made without meat, so meat flavor is absent, but by careful selection of raw materials, spices and binders, sausages of different color and flavor can be produced.

Color

In meat products the characteristic pink color is obtained by using sodium nitrite. Sodium nitrite (cure #1) reacts with meat myoglobin and after heat treatment the meat remains permanently pink. There is no myoglobin in vegetarian products, so adding nitrite will lead us nowhere. However, the color can be controlled by a smart selection of raw materials, spices, and protein emulsions.

Photo 1.5 Lentils - green, red, brown and French.

Advantages of Vegetarian Sausages

The sky is the limit when creating vegetarian sausages:

- Grains, nuts and beans come in all shapes and colors. Lentil can be green or pink, flaxseed gold or brown, quinoa white or red, cultivated rice is white, wild rice is black, and the list goes on. Potato flour is white, semolina yellow and pea flour green. Vegetarian sausages can be green, white, gray, pink, yellow, red or even blue with differently colored showpiece materials embedded into the binding paste of different colors.

- Vegetarian sausages can be sweet. Granola bar, peanut bar, energy bar-all those popular snacks can be made as sausages. A great benefit is that you control how much sugar and calories the sausage will have.

Photo 1.6 White, yellow and black wild rice.

Photo 1.7 Yellow and green peas.

Composition of a Vegetarian Sausage

There is a preconceived perception to how meat sausages should look and taste which is backed by hundreds of years of tradition. One could introduce raisins or cranberries into a liver sausage, grains into a blood sausage, or mix rice and potatoes with ground meat. There are well known classical meat sausages of this type, however, adding peanut butter, vanilla, honey, raisins and nuts in larger quantities will probably not be accepted because "this is not how the sausage should be made."

To extend their value sausages were made with additional materials such as barley, buckwheat, rice, oats, dry rolls or potatoes. Some blood sausages were made with a small amount of blood and grains. By removing the meat component from those sausages we create a vegetarian sausage. Food products continuously evolve and sometimes a customer reluctantly accepts new versions of classical dishes.

Take for example pizza - originally it was a thin dough crust with tomato sauce and cheese topping. Then we added pepperoni, sausage, bacon, spinach, broccoli, thicker crust, deep pan pizza, pineapples and ham toppings - there is no more standard for making pizza. Without a doubt some old timers frown upon such practices, but a new generation of creative cooks do not care. The original definition of the sausages has been distorted as well, the best example is McDonalds® where McDonalds® Sausage is a meat patty served on a bun. What does a meat patty have to do with a sausage? Following this reasoning further we may call a hamburger the sausage as well.

There are no such preconceived notions for vegetarian sausages and there are no standards. The field of making vegetarian sausages is open to all ideas and suggestions so let your imagination run loose. Think in terms of sausage evolution. There are pork sausages stuffed with raspberries, which is a logical progression as pork agrees with sweet toppings like apple sauce, cranberries or even mint sauce. We all know that baked ham tasted better if it was spiked with cloves and rubbed with brown sugar. How about honey glazed ham, such combinations were unheard of in the past.

As the definition of the sausage starts fading away, we have an interesting case of vegetarian sausages as there are no established rules that govern their manufacture. That means that any preconceived notion about making sausages does not apply here. The amount of salt or sodium nitrite, smoking and cooking temperatures are irrelevant, we can unleash our imagination and build them the way we like. Thus the definition of a vegetarian sausage becomes: *any food of non-animal origin that is stuffed into a non-animal casing.* With so much liberty why not make snack type sausages? Chinese are very fond of adding sugar to their sausages, so why not go one step further and create a snack type of the sausage. Energy bars are expensive vegetarian products - all you have to do is make them round and stuff into a clear casing and you have a snack sausage which was custom designed by you. It is a sure bet that your children would love the idea, ask them for help and you can create a snack that would be both tasty and healthy, unlike commercially sugar loaded products.

A typical vegetarian sausage consists of:

- **Principal (dominant) material:** grains, legumes, potatoes.
- **Protein source:** wheat gluten, tofu, textured vegetable protein (TVP).
- **Fat:** vegetable oil.
- **Binder:** flour, starch, natural gums, flaxseed emulsion.
- **Show material**: nuts, seeds, dry fruit, diced tofu, TVP.
- **Ingredients:** salt, sugar, honey, spices, natural colorings, vegetable stock.

Dominant material *names* the sausage - pea sausage, potato sausage, rice sausage. Those materials should be easily recognizable when the sausage is sliced, otherwise we end up with a hot dog type emulsified sausage which is a paste stuffed into a casing. TVP or tofu is added to many sausages but will have little bearing on the name of the sausage as it is added as a show material. When seeing the name Curry Sausage we already expect that curry will be the dominant spice, the flavor of garlic should be present in Garlic Sausage, and Green Pea Sausage should be of green color. The smoky flavor should be present in Smoked Sausage, White Sausage should be white and Vegetarian Blood Sausage should be reddish, even though no blood has been added.

Naming Vegetarian Sausages

Commercially produced vegetarian sausages are all of the same type: they are emulsified sausages like hot dog and their flavor is in a desperate need of improvement. All ingredients are dumped into a bowl cutter, which is a huge food processor, and a set of 3-4 knives rotate with an astonishing speed of a few thousand revolutions per minute. At the same time, the bowl containing all materials slowly rotates around. The knives, due to friction, will burn in no time, so to protect them about 30% of crushed ice or cold water is added. Then, this paste is filled into a casing. All those commercially produced veggie sausages include tofu, soy protein, gums and plenty of other ingredients.

A vegetarian sausage does not always need to be of the same diameter, display the same color, have the same emulsified texture and be made with tofu. There are hundreds of grains, flours, and starches which come in different shapes, sizes and color. There are seeds, dry fruits and nuts that can be utilized. Flours, starches and gums will easy bind grains and other components together. The sausage can look visually pleasing, it can have a great particle recognition, meat like chewy texture and great flavor. And it can be stuffed in different diameter casings.

The sausages in this book are named after the main filler material that was included in their composition. If barley was the main ingredient, the sausage is called Barley Sausage, if potatoes were the main filler it is called Potato Sausage, and so on: Quinoa Sausage, Lentil Sausage, Bean Sausage, Split Pea Sausage etc. Many of those sausages will contain tofu, wheat gluten or textured vegetable protein (TVP) as show material, in addition to the main material. Wheat gluten is probably the closest material which resembles the texture of meat, however, we have tried to limit its use in our recipes as many peaople are gluten sensitive.

The recipes were chosen for their academic value and originality, however, follow the quote below and feel free to improvise.

Let us quote Madame Benoit, the famous Canadian cookery expert and author who once said:

> *"I feel a recipe is only a theme, which an intelligent cook can play each time with a variation."*

The quote says it all - *improvise and create your own recipes. If you like your creation it must be a good sausage, if you have any doubts, try again.*

Food Safety

Non-animal materials provide less opportunity for pathogenic bacteria to grow, unlike meat which is a breeding ground for all types of bacteria. In addition meat and fish my be infected with worms and parasites which are not present in dry foods of vegetable nature. Food safety is nothing else but the control of bacteria. *Keeping them at low temperatures does not kill them, but only stops them from multiplying.* Once when the conditions are favorable again, they will wake up and start growing again.

Given favorable conditions bacteria can double up in numbers every 20 minutes. In a refrigerator their number will also grow, albeit at a reduced pace, but they can double up in 12 hours. Short of deep freezing, it is impossible to stop bacteria from contaminating food, but we can create conditions that will slow down their growing rate. At room temperatures bacteria will grow anywhere they have access to nutrients and water.

Under the correct conditions, spoilage bacteria reproduce rapidly and the populations can grow very large. Temperature and time are the factors that affect bacterial growth the most. Below 45° F (7° C) bacteria grow slowly and at temperatures above 140° F (60° C) they start to die. In the so called "danger zone" between 40-140° F (4-60° C) many bacteria grow very well. Most bacteria will grow exponentially at temperatures between 70° F (21° C) and 120° F (49° C). When bacteria grow, they increase in numbers, not in size.

After cooking, meats and other foods are free of bacteria, but leaving them warm for an extended time *will invite new bacteria* to settle in and start growing. For this reason smoked and subsequently cooked meats are submitted to cold showers to pass through the "danger zone" as fast as possible. The only way to kill bacteria and make food safe is by thorough cooking.

Gluten

All grains contain protein known as gluten, but people with celiac disease and most other gluten allergies only react to gluten found in *wheat, barley, and rye* and products derived from those grains.

Gluten Intolerance

If you suspect that you react badly to gluten - with symptoms like diarrhea, upset stomach, abdominal pain, and bloating - get tested for celiac disease, all it takes is a blood test. If you have celiac disease and you eat gluten, the lining of your small intestine becomes inflamed and gets damaged, making it harder for your body to absorb nutrients. That can lead to malnutrition and weight loss. Many people do not have celiac disease, but are very sensitive to ingesting gluten.

The common symptoms include gastrointestinal problems, joint pain, fatigue and depression.

Murphy's Law states: *"if it's not broken, don't fix it."*

So don't go on a gluten free diet when there is no need for it. Let your body work the way it was designed to. Gluten-free diets *do help* people who are *sensitive* to gluten. There's a misconception that a gluten-free diet helps with other conditions or with weight loss. Whole grains are an important part of a healthy diet and a gluten-free diet offers no health-related benefits for people who do not suffer from gluten intolerance.

Equipment

Grinders are tool that are indispensable for making meat sausages, however, they are less important for making vegetarian sausages. Most vegetarian sausages are made from precooked grains or soaked materials that do not need to be ground, only occasionally a recipe will call for grinding wheat gluten.

Photo 1.8 Sausage Maker's stainless steel #10 manual grinder.

Sausage Stuffer

The sausage stuffer is probably the most important tool that you should carry. Sausages must be filled very firmly and the stuffer is a must tool for the job. There are two choices: a manual grinder with a stuffing tube attachment and a piston stuffer.

Photo 1.9 Grinder with an attached stuffing tube.

Fig. 1.10 Stuffing tubes.

Although a manual grinder with an attached stuffing tube is an awkward arrangement for a single person to handle, it works surprisingly well with vegetarian sausages. It is a good machine to process smaller batches of sausages in the range of 2-5 pounds. You may start with a manual grinder, but if you intend to make 5 pounds of sausage or more, then upgrade to a 5 pounds piston stuffer. The reason that the piston stuffer is less suitable for making small amounts of sausages is that there is always some leftover material remaining under the piston when the stuffing is done. A large 15 lb stuffer has a large diameter cylinder so more material will remain. Get a 5 lb capacity model which is a perfect size machine for most jobs.

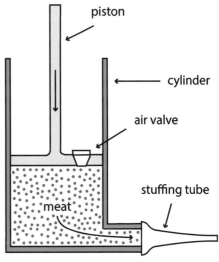

Photo 1.11 5 lb stuffer manufactured by the Sausage Maker is an ideal machine for making small batches of sausages.

www.sausagemaker.com

Fig. 1.1 Piston stuffer.

Cutting and Blending Equipment

A good knife, food processor/blender will take care of general tasks and making emulsions. Don't underestimate the power of a manual wisk which is a wonderful tool for blending and is easy to clean. A small 100 g (3.5 oz) test sausage may call for 50 g of emulsion. There is no way that even a small processor will process such a small amount of food as its knives are positioned too high. You can, however, do it easily with a wisk. In addition the wisk works slower so you can introduce last minute changes and you can see the changes as they occur.

Photo 1.12 Blender.   **Photo 1.13** Food processor.   **Photo 1.14** Whisk and bowl.

Photo 1.15 Spice mill/grinder.

Usually it is possible to purchase ground seeds such as flaxseeds, however, some seeds for example poppy seeds may require you to grind yourself.

Measuring is accomplished with common kitchen tools like cups, spoons and scales.

Photo 1.16 Measuring cup.

Photo 1.17 100 ml measuring cylinder is a must have tool for control of small amounts of liquid. Having a second, smaller 10 ml capacity will be helpful too.

In addition to a general kitchen scale which is accurate to 1 g, a highly accurate digital scale is needed for measuring small amounts of gums and spices.

Photo 1.18 AWS CD-V2-100 digital scale has 100 g capacity and is accurate to 0.01 g (0.001 oz).

Making Test Sausages

Let's say you come up with a new idea for a sausage. Although the composition might seem unusual at the first glance, you will never know how it will taste until it is made. It will not be practical to cook 5 pounds of oats and mix them with 1 pound of honey, a half pound of raisins and so on. However, you can make a test sausage within 30 minutes and this will proof your recipe.

Assembling a grinder and stuffer to make 3.5 oz of test sausage is not practical as it requires much subsequent cleaning. It is simpler attach the casing to a suitable funnel and stuff the sausage mass manually as depicted in the photographs below.

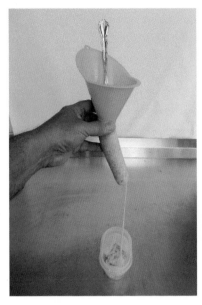

Photos 1.19-1.21 Stuffing sausages with a funnel.

The picture below depicts a set up for stuffing a larger 51 mm diameter casing. From the left: a casing, stainless steel Sausage Maker 1-1/8" tube for 5 lb stuffer, yellow funnel, 10" long 1" diameter piece of broom stick which acts as a pusher.

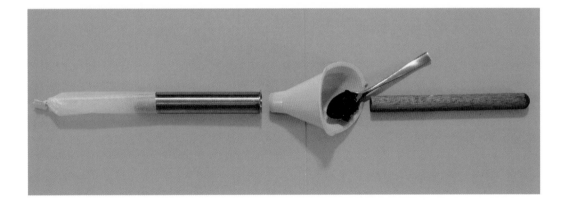

Photo 1.22 Stuffing funnel.

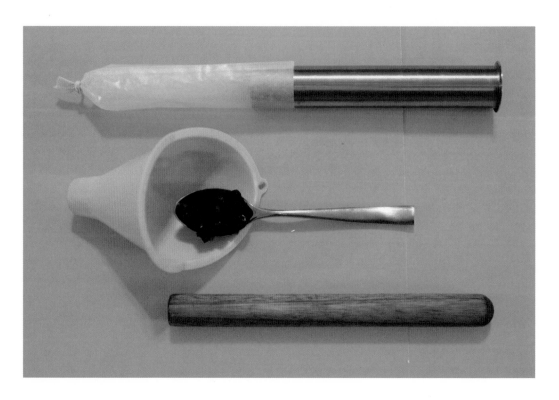

Photo 1.23 Stuffing funnel.

Photo 1.24 Traditional manual funnel stuffer.

A small amount of sausage can be stuffed using the above set up faster than assembling the stuffer. The clean up is a snap and no problems with storage space. After a few sessions you learn when to release the casing when pushing down the pusher stick. This is how the sausages were stuffed in the past.

Casings

Casings are divided into two categories:

- Natural - pigs, sheep, goats, cattle and sometimes horses. Kosher sausages will not be stuffed into hog casings.

- Artificial - collagen, cellulose, or even plastic. Artificial casings from animal collagen can be edible, depending on the origin of the raw material. Collagen casings with a diameter of 32 mm or more are usually not edible.

Collagen casings are produced from the collagen in beef or pig hides, and the bones and tendons. It can also be derived from poultry and fish. In any case they do not meet the requirements of pure vegans.

Cellulose, usually from cotton linters or wood pulp, is processed to make viscose which is then extruded into clear, tough casings. Cellulose skinless casings are manufactured in shirred sticks that do not require soaking. They are highly permeable for excellent smoke absorption and color. They have tiny little holes that allow smoke and moisture to go through. This in our experiments created a problem as the flour was leaking through.

Synthetic casings are made of synthetic thermoplastic materials and are mechanically strong.

The Sausage Maker Inc., offers a variety of casings suitable for vegetarian sausages.

Photo 1.25 Clear fibrous casings pictured on the right are offered in diameters from 38 mm (1.5") to 88 mm (3-3/8"). The casings should be soaked for 30 minutes in water before use. Plastic casings depicted below do not need soaking.

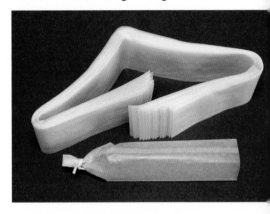

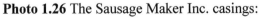

Photo 1.26 The Sausage Maker Inc. casings:
Top: 38 mm clear fibrous
Middle: 32 mm curved plastic
Bottom: 26 mm curved plastic

Photo 1.27 Sausages stuffed into casings which are presented in the Photo 1.26 on the left.

Chapter Summary

It is probably fair to assume that people attempting to make vegetarian sausages are lacking basic sausage making skills. Those skills are usually acquired by making a variety of meat sausages such as smoked sausages, head cheeses, liver and blood sausages or fermented sausages like pepperoni or salami. The sausage maker must deal with curing meat, development of color, pre-freezing fat for a clean cut, safe cooking temperatures and a lot of regulations. Making vegetarian sausages falls into the general cooking area and is much easier and safer. However, if we call the product "sausage" it should look and feel like one.

A vegetarian stays away from meat and natural animal casings so he starts to improvise with parchment paper or foil as a substitute material for animal casings. Those methods, however, will not produce a tightly stuffed sausage. It will be better to use the archaic methods from the past and stuff the synthetic casing through a funnel. There is of course no substitute for a manually operated piston stuffer.

There are countless recipes on the Internet that call for stuffing vegetarian sausages into parchment paper or foil. We can understand someone making Nham fermented sausage in the middle of the Thai jungle who uses banana leaves to wrap up his sausage, but we live in the USA, so why not to use proper casings?

The sausage stuffer applies more pressure than we could ever attempt with our fingers and synthetic casings are strong and permeable to smoke and moisture. To sum up the discussion there is plenty of inexpensive equipment and supplies that can and should be used in order to produce high quality vegetarian sausages.

Photo 1.28 Polenta sausage with raisins and cranberries.

Chapter 2

Materials and Ingredients

The Importance of Fat

One of the characteristics of fat is that it acts as a flavor intensifier. In addition, fat provides a pleasant mouthfeel which is hard to replace with fat substitutes. People find a low-fat diet bland and have difficulty to maintain it over a period of time. To function properly our body needs fat. It maintains cell membranes, absorbs vitamins, carries food flavors and provides energy. Fats can be classified as:

- Saturated - found mainly in animals (meat and poultry, butter, cheese and milk products). Cocoa butter, coconut oil and palm oil are also highly saturated. Saturated fats are solid at room temperature: lard, butter, suet. Saturated fats are "bad fats."
- Monounsaturated fat - found in plants, but also in animals. Olive, canola and peanut oil. These are "good fats."
- Polyunsaturated fat-plants. Corn, olive, canola, peanut, sunflower, soybean, safflower, cotton seed. Also present in fish. These are "good fats."

Oils

Oils are the fats which are used in vegetarian sausages. They are liquid at room temperature and low in saturated fatty acids. *Oils are generally much healthier* and contain less saturated acids. The fats in seafood, nuts, and seeds are considered oils.

Comparative properties of common cooking oils per 1 Tbsp (14g)				
	Total Fat	Saturated Fat	Monounsaturated Fat	Polyunsaturated Fat
Canola	14 g	1.0 g	8.0 g	4.0 g
Corn	14 g	2.0 g	4.0 g	8.0 g
Olive	14 g	2.0 g	10.0 g	1.5 g
Soy	14 g	2.2 g	3.20 g	8.0 g
Sunflower	14 g	1.5 g	3.0 g	9.0 g
Peanut	14 g	2.5 g	6.0 g	5.0 g
None of the oils contain trans fat, sodium, protein or cholesterol.				

All fats, oils included go "rancid" (deterioration of flavor) in time even when frozen, however, in oils the rancidity starts to develop after one year. Adding directly more than 5% oil to a vegetarian sausage can make it oily and greasy, however, larger amounts can be added in the form of emulsion as explained in Chapter 4.

Additives used in sausage production can be classified as:

1. Extenders and binders. These products extend expensive meat proteins with cheaper plant proteins, like soy proteins. Non-fat dry milk, sodium caseinate (milk protein) and egg white fit into this category too. The main purpose of using meat extenders has been to lower the cost of a product. They are capable of binding water as well. A mixture of *three parts water and one part vegetable protein* is prepared and this paste can be added to ground meat. A typical proportion: 75% meat, 25% extender. Such an extender can be added to vegan sausages, however, protein-water-oil emulsion is a better choice. The most commonly used extenders are:

- Soy protein isolate (SPI), see Chapter 3.
- Soy protein concentrate (SPC), see Chapter 3.
- Sodium caseinate, see Chapter 4.
- Whey protein, see Chapter 4

The above products augment the protein content of the sausage, however, the main reason for their use is their ability to provide *binding, emulsifying and extending properties.* This improves texture, color and flavor of the sausages.

2. Fillers - increase the volume of the sausage. The result is a lower cost yet still nutritive product. Fillers are carbohydrate products able to absorb large quantities of water but they are not good emulsifiers. Fillers are usually added at 2-15%. By using meat extenders and fillers together, the cost of the extended product can be lowered significantly.

- **Grains** - amaranth, barley, buckwheat, corn, millet, oats, quinoa, rye, rice, sorghum, teff, wheat.
- **Roots and Tubers** - potatoes, cassava, taro, yams, beets.
- **Legumes** are among the best protein sources.: beans, peas, lentils, peanuts.

3. Emulsions. See Chapter 4.

4. Gums immobilize water and contribute viscosity. This improves texture, sliceability and provides better mouthfeel.

5. Binders

Egg white is often added to sausages to increase binding of ingredients. It should be noted that only the egg white possesses binding properties. The egg yolk is a *good emulsifier* but contributes to more cholesterol and calories.

Egg (100 g serving)	Protein (g)	Fat (g)	Carbohydrates (g)	Salt (mg)	Energy (cal)	Cholesterol (mg)
Egg Whole, raw	12.56	9.51	0.72	142	143	372
Egg White, raw	10.90	0.17	0.73	166	52	0
						Source: USDA Nutrient database

Egg white is often added (1-3%) to frankfurters with low meat content. It increases protein content, *forms stable gel and contributes to a firm texture of the sausage*. Powdered egg whites are also available and you generally mix 2 teaspoons of powder with 2 tablespoons of water for each white.

Ingredient (100 g serving)	Protein (g)	Fat (g)	Carbohydrates (g)	Salt (mg)	Energy (cal)
Egg, white, dried	81.10	0.00	7.80	1280	382
					Source: USDA Nutrient database

Ready to use liquid egg *whites* that are packaged in convenient size containers are available in supermarkets.

Ingredient (46 g serving)	Protein (g)	Fat (g)	Carbohydrates (g)	Salt (mg)	Energy (cal)
Egg, white, liquid	5	0.00	0.00	75	25
					Source: Crystal Farms, All Whites®

From Bob's Red Mill:

Egg Replacer: 1 Tbsp Bob's Red Mill Flaxseed Meal + 3 Tbsp water = 1 egg.

Mix Bob's Red Mill flaxseed meal and water in a small bowl and let sit for one to two minutes. Add to a recipe as you would an egg. This is a very versatile egg replacement formula.

Non-fat dry milk is produced by removing fat and water from milk. Lactose (milk sugar), milk proteins and milk minerals are present in the same relative proportions as in fresh milk. Dry milk powder greatly *improves the taste of low fat sausages*. It is added at about 3% and effectively binds water and emulsifies fats. Its action is very similar to that of soy protein concentrate.

Ingredient (100 g serving)	Protein (g)	Fat (g)	Carbohydrates (g)	Salt (mg)	Energy (cal)
Non-fat dry milk	36.16	0.77	51.98	535	362
					Source: USDA Nutrient database

Gelatin

Gelatin, technically classified as a hydrocolloid is made from by-products of the meat and leather industry (bones, hides, pig skin). When mixed with water, it forms a semi-solid colloid gel. Gelatin forms a thermoreversible gel - it melts to a liquid when heated and solidifies when cooled again. Gelatin may be used as a stabilizer, or thickener in foods such as jams, yoghurt, cream cheese, and margarine. It is used in fat-reduced foods to mimic the mouthfeel of fat and to increase volume without adding calories. Combining gelatin with various hydrocolloids has resulted in new food additives that closely mimic the mouthfeel of fats.

Ingredient (100 g serving)	Protein (g)	Fat (g)	Carbohydrates (g)	Salt (mg)	Energy (cal)
Gelatin, dry powder	85.60	0.10	0.00	196	335

Source: USDA Nutrient database

Powdered gelatin added at 1-2% helps to bind de-boned meat together or stuffing individual cuts of meat which are not perfectly lean. Gelatin is widely used in meat products for decorative jellies for pates and for the coating and glazing of ham and other cooked meat products giving these products an attractive appearance. Gelatin also improves the slicing characteristics of meats by penetrating and filling any cavities in the meat tissue, especially where the bone has been removed. This bonds individual meat pieces together which is of crucial importance when making molded hams.

Gelatin is also used in the manufacture of canned meat products where it serves to absorb the juices that are released during the retorting process. Gelatin being almost pure protein also enhances the protein balance of the final product. Gelatin is first dispersed in cold water and then completely dissolved in water at 122-140° F (50-60° C). Gelatin is a much more powerful thickener than egg. Gelatin is always used in a ratio to liquids in the recipe: usually 1/4 ounce of powdered gelatin is needed to set 16 ounces of liquid. To obtain a "semi-solid" consistency increase the liquid to 32 ounces. If the ratio is incorrect, the product will be either runny or too firm and rubbery.

Fillers

Beans make a good filler and can act as a showpiece material. Red or black beans will look striking against a background of white protein emulsion. Everybody likes burritos which is ground meat mixed with bean paste. How about chili? Beans can be soaked in water for a few hours then simmered in a little water. The resulting bean paste can be used as a filler.

Bread crumbs are ground and roasted bread particles. They absorb water very well, similarly to rusk. Bread crumbs can absorb water at 2 times their weight.

Barley and buckwheat groats are added to many sausages, for example to Polish blood sausages, however, they are suitable as a filler material for any sausage.

Buckwheat groats are cooked for about 20 minutes in water as follows:

1 part *raw buckwheat* groats to 1.8 part water
1 part *roasted raw buckwheat* groats to 2 parts water
1 part *barley groats* to 2.1 parts of water

Roasted buckwheat groats are much darker in color, have more intense flavor and are less popular for making sausages.

Cracker meal is a type of coarse flour which is made from finely milled crackers. Cracker meal is used for breading meat or fish or topping dishes to be baked or broiled. Cracker meal is similar to bread crumbs, although it is lighter in color and has a milder taste. It can absorb water at 1.5 times its weight.

Dried Wheat Rolls

After World War II ended in Europe people in heavily damages countries like Poland, Russia or Germany could not buy bread crumbs in stores because there were no stores. They would save and dry wheat rolls. Then they would be soaked in water or milk and used as a filler in meat products.

You can save wheat rolls such as Portuguese rolls or French baguettes. They will dry out and will remain usable for a long time. Before use, soak them in water or milk. Then mix with ground meat and other ingredients. Add an egg to combine the mass better.

Photo 2.1 These rolls, known as Portuguese rolls, are widely available and dry perfectly.

Photo 2.2 A selection of grains, flours and starches.

Flours and Starches

Flours and starches make great fillers, water absorbers and binders. Flours such as corn, potato, wheat, soy and rice are in common use in the Western world. However, there are tubers such as cassava that grow in very hot climates in Africa, South America or the Caribbean region. The Caribbean and the nations with populations of West African origin such as Cuba, the Dominican Republic and Puerto Rico often use mashed plantains or yams which are then combined with other ingredients. Popular products are gari and tufu flour. Flours give the sausages a somewhat firmer structure. In sausages starch is used for its properties to bind water and to improve the texture of the product. The most common sources of starch are potato, wheat, corn, rice and tapioca. You can add as much flour as you like, but around 2-10% is added to meat sausages. Starch is a common additive in extended injected products like a ham. It is usually applied at 1-5% (10-50 g/kg) of a finished product. The amount of flour or starch can be increased in vegetarian sausages.

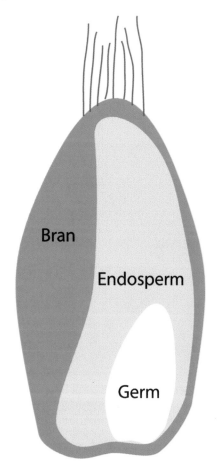

Bran is an outside beneficial fiber. It accounts for about 14.5% of the kernel weight.

Endosperm is a source of white flour. It accounts for about 83% of the kernel weight.

Germ is the embryo of the seed and accounts for 2.5% of the kernel weight.

Whole grains foods or whole grain flour must contain all three parts of the grain.

White flour is made from endosperm only. To compensate for the nutrients that were in bran and germ but were milled out, new nutrients are mixed with white flour and the product becomes *enriched white flour.*

Fig. 2.1 A kernel of wheat.

Flour is a thickener with half the thickening power of starch. There are many ways to use flour as a thickener – dredge stew meats in flour before browning it and the flour will later thicken the stew when a liquid is added. You can mix flour with a little cool liquid to form a paste and then add it into simmering sauce. One thing we shouldn't do with flour is throw it directly into hot liquid because the flour particles will clump together. To achieve full thickening power and eliminate raw flour taste, flour-thickened mixtures must be brought to a boil and then cooked for about 3 minutes. There is no need to cook longer because *flour thickens more as it cools*; as a rule stop cooking gravies and sauces when they're a bit thinner than their ideal consistency.

Nutritional Values of Different Flours (100 g serving)						
Name	Protein (g)	Fat (g)	Carbohydrates (g)	Salt (mg)	Fiber (g)	Calories (cal)
Soy, full-fat	34.54	20.65	35.19	13	9.6	436
Soy, low-fat	45.51	8.90	34.93	9	16.0	375
Soy, de-fatted	47.01	1.22	38.37	20	17.5	330
Wheat, whole grain	13.21	2.50	71.97	2	10.7	340
Wheat, white	10.33	0.98	76.31	2	2.7	364
Potato	6.90	0.34	83.10	55	5.9	357
Rice, white	5.95	1.42	80.13	0	2.4	366
Corn, whole grain, white	6.93	3.86	76.85	5	7.3	361
Semolina	12.68	1.05	72.83	1	3.9	360
Chickpea (besan)	22.39	6.69	57.82	64	10.8	387
Source: USDA Nutrient database						

Corn flour, (maize, corn meal) contributes to good slicing characteristics. Corn flour comes in yellow and white and is used for breading and in combination with other flours in baked goods White corn flour blends well with other food ingredients and can be blended with wheat flour.

Gram flour is a flour made from ground chickpeas. It is also known as chickpea flour, garbanzo flour, or besan. In comparison to other common flours such as wheat, potato, rice, corn, and semolina, it has a relatively high proportion of protein. Used in many countries, it is a staple ingredient in Indian, Pakistani and Bangladeshi cuisines, and in the form of a paste with water or yoghurt. Moreover, when mixed with an equal proportion of water it can be used as an egg-replacer in vegan cooking. Chila (or chilla), a pancake made with gram flour batter is a popular street and fast food in India.

Green pea flour is made by grinding green peas. High in protein and fiber, it is an excellent addition to baked goods, soups, sauces and dips.

Polenta is cornmeal made into a porridge by cooking ground yellow corn. The term is of Italian origin, however, it can be found all over the world in the form of maize porridge. Polenta has a creamy texture due to the gelatinization of starch in the grain. It can be ground coarsely or finely depending on the texture desired, however, creamier polenta is produced with a fine grind. Polenta was originally classified as a peasant food, after all, it is ground corn. In recent years polenta has found popularity as a gourmet food. Many current polenta recipes enrich polenta with meat and mushroom sauces, and add vegetables, beans or various cheeses into the basic mixture. Not surprisingly, polenta can be used with great success in vegetarian sausages.

Polenta takes a long time to cook, typically simmering in four to five times its volume in water for about 45 minutes with almost constant stirring needed for even gelatinization of the starch. Cooked polenta must be thick enough to be shaped into balls, patties, or sticks, and then fried in oil, baked, or grilled until golden brown. Polenta porridge can be eaten with milk for breakfast.

Potato flour is the preferred flour for making meat sausages. Many Russian sausages include around 2-3% of potato flour in their composition. It made sausages cheaper and improved the mouthfeel of low fat products. Potato flour binds water well and has flavor that agrees quite well with reduced-fat sausages improving their texture and mouthfeel. It is a good filler for vegetarian sausages.

Rice flour is made milling white or brown rice. Rice flour may be used as a thickening agent in recipes that are refrigerated or frozen since it inhibits liquid separation. It is a good substitute for wheat flour.

Semolina is made during the grinding of harder durum wheat to make flour. Healthy high caloric food (325 cal per 100 g) semolina was often given with milk and sugar to children for breakfast. Semolina is used in making pasta, breakfast cereals, puddings, bread crust and general baking.

Durum wheat is considered the top choice for making paste; the wheat kernel's density and high protein and gluten content result in firm pasta with a consistent cooking quality and golden color. In sausages it is used to bind ingredients together. Semolina contributes to a stronger binding and has been used as a filler in many European sausages, for example Polish Semolina Liver Sausage, Jowl Sausage and Blood Head Cheese.

Photo 2.3 Green pea flour. **Photo 2.4** Potato flour. **Photo 2.5** Semolina flour.

Soy flour. All flours can be used for making vegetarian sausages, although soy flour may impart a "beany taste" to the product.

Tapioca starch and tapioca flour are *the same thing*. Tapioca is a pure starch derived from the root of the *cassava* plant and it comes in many forms. The small granules of pearl tapioca are widely available and work well as a thickener. Tapioca gel is crystal clear and has a strong jelly-like consistency.

Wheat flour is made from the grinding of wheat. More wheat flour is produced than any other flour and there are specialized flours for cake, bread and pasta making. General purpose flour is the most popular type.

In addition to typical flours that we are accustomed to, there is a great variety of flours that are utilized in tropical countries, for example African gari and tufu flours are made from yam or cassava flour is made from cassava (yuca). They can be easily obtained online.

Starch and Starch Derived Products

Starch is made by most plants for use as an energy. Ready to eat foods containing starch are bread, pancakes, cereals, noodles, pasta, porridge and tortilla. All starches are good thickeners and are used to thicken soups or gravies. In general baking, especially in pastry filling starch plays an important role as it is such a strong gelling agent. Starch has the ability to swell and take on water. Varying the ratio of starch to water will change its properties. The swelling of the starch occurs during the heating stage. *As a starch paste cools a gel is formed.* All starches begin to thicken at around 140° F (60° C). However, to achieve full thickening power, cereal flour and starch which have a high percentage of a starch molecule called amylose must come all the way to a boil and be held just below the boiling point for several minutes to cook off the raw starch flavor. *Potato starch* thickens quickly without a pronounced flavor that needs to be cooked off which makes it great as a last minute fix for too-thin sauces. Its ability to gel below water boiling temperature made it popular with meat sausages. Adding starch directly into the cooking food will form lumps that are then difficult to dissolve. To avoid lumps mix the starch with an equal amount of cold liquid until it forms a paste, then whisk it into the liquid to thicken it. Starch is made of two main components:

- Amylose.
- Amylopectin – contributes towards a strong, translucent, stringy gel.

When water is added and it is heated some of the bonds between the amylase and amylopectin molecules break and the starch undergoes "gelatinization," which means it becomes gel. The properties of starch (and gel) depend on the ratio of amylase and amylopectin.

Starch comes from:

- Roots/tubers – potato, arrowroot, tapioca. Roots/tubers contain about 80% amylopectin
- Cereal – corn, wheat, rice. Cereals contain about 75%, however, rice contains almost all amylopectin and very little amylase.

Starches		
Roots/ Tubers	Arrow-root	Rich in amylopectin, thicken well before the boiling point, makes a clear gel.
	Tapioca	Rich in amylopectin, thickens well before the boiling point. Makes clean gel, freezes well. Tapioca starch and tapioca flour are the same thing.
	Potato	*Rich in amylopectin, best thickening ability. Sets at relatively low temperature, does not need to go into a boil. It produces very clear gel, softer than corn starch.*
Cereals	Corn	Corn starch contains less amylopectin than potato starch so it is a less effective thickening agent than potato starch, however, it produces a strong gel. It must be heated to higher temperatures than potato starch.
	Rice	Rice starch has the smallest particle size of all starches making it very absorbent. It has a very clean taste and doesn't interfere with other flavors. Rice starch is often used in baby formulas.
	Wheat	Worst thickening ability. It thickens at boiling temperature and must be thoroughly cooked.

Cornstarch is derived from corn. It can withstand a good amount of cooking and stirring before it begins to break down. That's why it's frequently used for thickening pastry products which are baked or foods which are cooked on the stove and involve prolonged heating and stirring. Cornstarch has twice the thickening power of flour, but like flour it imparts a slightly starchy taste which disappears after a few minutes of high heating. Another advantage is that unlike flour-thickened sauces it doesn't separate when frozen.

Arrowroot starch comes from the root of a tropical plant of the same name. Look for it in gourmet or health-food stores. Arrowroot starch granules are very small and make sauces exceptionally smooth. Like flour and cornstarch it can withstand long cooking and higher temperatures, and like tapioca it is remarkable for its clarity. It's a great choice for stir-fry sauces and any kind of fruit pie filling.

In food applications a starch is twice as effective as the flour it was made from.

Flour	Equivalent Amount of Starch			
	Corn	Tapioca	Arrowroot	Potato
2 Tbsp	1 Tbsp	1 Tbsp	1 Tbsp plus 1-1/2 tsp	1-1/2 tsp

Potato starch is most commonly called for in European recipes. It's easy to find in the baking ingredient aisle of East Coast markets, but in the rest of the country look for it in the kosher section of the store. Potato starch is 100 percent starch whereas potato flour is about 85 percent starch, the rest being largely fiber, protein, fat, and sugar. Potato starch is pure white, while potato flour is yellowish having traces of color and flavor from the potato. Potato starch turns clear while potato flour turns opaque. To extract the starch the potatoes are crushed and the starch grains are released from the mashed potatoes. The starch is then washed out and dried to powder. The superior water binding of potato starches improves moisture retention and increases yield while providing juiciness in processed meats.

Potato Starch	Potato Flour
A very fine flour, neutral taste, made by removing potato skin, then made into a watery slurry, and dehydrated to form potato starch powder. It is not cooked and it *does not absorb much water, unless it is heated*. When heated with liquid, it will make an excellent sauce or gravy.	Potato flour is made from the potato, including the skin and it is cooked. It has a slight potato flavor. Potato flour contains protein, the starch does not. It can absorb large amounts of liquid.

Unmodified potato starch gelatinizes at 147° F (64° C) which is below the recommended meat internal temperature for cooked food so a strong gel is always assured. Other starches gelatinize at temperatures from 165° F (73° C) to 178° F (81° C).

100 g serving	Protein (g)	Fat (g)	Carbohydrates (g)	Salt (mg)	Energy (cal)	Cholesterol (mg)
Potato flour	8.82	1.47	79.4	0	353	0
Potato starch	0	0	83.3	0	333	0
					Source: Bob's Red Mill Natural Foods	

Photo 2.6 Potato flour left, starch on the right. Both were mixed with 4 parts of water, then heated.

Photo 2.7 Potato starch produces a very clear gel.

What is Better for Sausages – the Flour or the Starch?

All starches begin to thicken at around 140° F (60° C). But to achieve full thickening power flour cereal starches (corn, rice, wheat) need to be heated to 212° F (100° C) which makes them less suited for making sausages. Meat sausages, liver, blood or head cheese, whether smoked are usually boiled in water at 176° F (80° C) until the meat reaches around 160° F (72° C) temperature inside. If the temperature is higher, the fat melts, the texture and quality suffers and the sausage is greasy on the outside. Potato starch is a root starch and root starches gel below the boiling point (212° F, 100° C). Many Russian and Polish sausages included around 2% *potato flour* in their composition. Not wheat, rye, corn or rice flour, but the potato flour. Swedish sausages are made with potatoes and they are delicious. Well, if potato flour and potato starch are so suitable for meat sausages, they should work well in vegetarian sausages as well.

It takes twice as much flour as starch to create a gel. Take for example tofu which is soft and contains plenty of water. Using too much tofu will make your sausage very soft. Adding starch or gum will bind some water, but the resulting gel will be soft as well. However, more flour is needed than starch to bind water so the sausage will be much firmer. Gelled flour produces an opaque paste unlike a clear gel made from starch. If you want to create a white sausage with clearly visible ingredients such as cranberries or pistachios, it may be better to use a starch. If the color is less important, flour is a better filler material.

A combination of *starch and gum* produces a synergistic effect:

- starch and carrageenan.
- 1 part potato starch and 2 parts of guar gum.
- 1 part potato flour and 3 parts guar gum.

For making sausages potato flour is the best choice as it has a great flavor, gels at low temperature and does not contain gluten, a fact to consider by people allergic to it.

Rusk is a popular filler in England. It is made from wheat flour mixed with water, *baked* and crushed. It can be ground to different diameters and there is a coarse, medium or fine rusk. It is a good binder and can absorb water at 3 - 4 times its weight.

Textured Vegetable Protein (TVP) is a great filler - described in Chapter 3.

Vital wheat gluten is all gluten and very little starch. It is is made from the protein found in the endosperm of the wheat berry, containing 75% to 80% protein by hydrating the flour to activate the gluten and then processed to remove everything but that gluten.

It is then dried and ground back into a powder. It is responsible for the stretchiness of dough and for the shapes that baked goods hold. Most baking sources recommend about one tablespoon for every 2-3 cups of flour.

Vital wheat gluten, 100 g serving					
Protein (g)	Fat (g)	Carbohydrates (g)	Salt (mg)	Energy (cal)	Cholesterol
55.5	0	33.3	0	388	0
					Source: Arrowhead Mills

Vital wheat gluten is also a staple ingredient for meat and meat substitutes. It acts as a *binder* for meatballs, meatloaf, veggie burgers and tofu alike. When the gluten dough is cooked, it becomes chewy with a meat-like texture, however, it has a very rubbery feel. In our trials we have obtained much better results making wheat gluten from whole wheat flour, although the process is more labor intensive. However, vital wheat gluten is a wonderful binder for many grains and other fillers like for example bread crumbs.

Fillers (Meat Substitutes)

The following soy materials can be considered main fillers, however, they are usually described as meat substitutes:

- Tofu, see Chapter 3.
- Wheat gluten also known as seitan.
- Tempeh, see Chapter 3.

We feel hesitant to call soy derived products "meat substitutes or analogues" because they cannot mimic the flavor of the meat so such a definition is wishful at best. It is better to break with the notion that vegetarian sausages should duplicate the flavor of meat sausages and think of them rather as a different type of sausage. A meat sausage is a meat sausage and a vegetarian sausage is a vegetarian sausage, two different products like apples and oranges. By accepting this fact we can remove the preconceived notion of how the sausage should be made, look or taste and free our imagination to create original vegetarian sausages.

Tofu - is the best known meat substitute, however, it does not really have a "meaty" texture, like wheat gluten or textured vegetable protein. Tofu is described in Chapter 3.

Wheat Gluten

Wheat gluten also called seitan, wheat meat, gluten meat, or simply gluten, is made from gluten, the main protein of wheat. It is made by kneading wheat flour dough in water until all the starch particles have been removed, leaving the sticky insoluble gluten paste which is then cooked before being eaten. Wheat gluten is not a good choice for celiacs and gluten-sensitive individuals so it is less popular than tofu, however, it displays the superior ability to take on the texture and flavor of meat. It can be thinly sliced on vegetarian sandwiches, added to sauces or used as topping on vegetarian pizza. Wheat gluten has a chewy texture that resembles meat more than other substitutes.

Photo 2.8 It may look like meat, but this is a solid chunk of wheat gluten made from whole wheat flour and vegetable broth.

Making Wheat Gluten

The procedure is simple; dough is made by combining whole wheat flour with water, then it is kneaded under to rinse away the starch. What is left is a high protein gluten dough. When the gluten dough is steamed, baked, or boiled, it becomes chewy with a meat like texture.

Making Wheat Gluten Traditional Method

Materials: whole wheat flour, water.

Place flour in a bowl. Add 50% water and start mixing, more water will be needed. For 1 lb (453 g) flour you may need around 1 cup and 1 oz of water (280 ml.

Photo 2.9 left: freshly made dough, right: the same dough after kneading for 20 minutes.

Photo 2.10 Kneaded dough. Left: general purpose flour. Middle: 1/2 general purpose plus 1/2 whole wheat flour. Right: whole wheat flour. Whole wheat flour produces the best texture, general purpose flour the worst, too soft and watery.

Photo 2.11 Cover the dough in water and leave it in the refrigerator overnight.

Photo 2.12 Next day fill the bowl with water and let run a little water from the faucet. Start kneading.

Break the dough into 2 inch diameter balls (it will be difficult to knead the whole piece of dough). Knead each ball for about 5 minutes underwater. This will force starch out and the water will become milky. Empty and refill the bowl periodically until the water stays clear. The dough will shrink to less than half its original size and get stretchy.

Photo 2.13 Starch free dough resembles a sponge.

Photo 2.14 Kneaded dough ready for cooking.

Photo 2.15 Bring a pot of water to a boil and drop the pieces of dough inside. Simmer for about 2 hours, the dough will swell.

Photo 2.16 It is done.

Photo 2.17 Wheat gluten can be sliced thinly.

Photo 2.18 Powdered annatto was added to dough and made the gluten red.

Making wheat gluten using shortcut method

Materials: *vital wheat gluten*, water.

Place vital wheat gluten flour in a bowl, add some water and mix. Start kneading adding water only if needed. Separate the gluten dough into smaller chunks and flatten them. Bring water or vegetable stock to a boil. The dough will expand so have enough liquid in a pot. Simmer covered for 2 hours. Remove from liquid and allow to cool. It is done when firm and expanded.

Photo 2.19 Wheat gluten made from vital wheat gluten four.

Photo 2.20 Wheat gluten can be sliced or ground like meat.

Photo 2.21 Vital wheat gluten flour makes very crumbly rubbery wheat gluten as seen at the bottom of the plate.

Discussion

- *Whole wheat flour produces the best gluten* with meat like bite and texture.
- Mixing whole wheat with general purpose flour has produced an *acceptable* product.
- General purpose flour produces very soft gluten.
- Using vital wheat gluten flour allows a faster method of making gluten, however, the product has a very *rubbery* texture that does not feel like meat at all. It is not suitable for grinding and its rubbery structure makes it a poor choice for sausages. This, however, does not diminish the exceptional value of vital wheat flour for general binding purposes.
- One pound of whole wheat flour will produce a little less than one pound of wheat gluten after cooking.
- Vegetable broth and flavorings can be added to dough, but keep in mind that whole wheat flour is kneaded extensively under water to remove starch, so there will be a significant loss of broth and spices. However, gluten will acquire flavor when boiled in a spiced vegetable broth.
- Wheat gluten freezes well.
- Wheat gluten can be diced and added as show material to other sausages.

Seitan

Seitan is flavored wheat gluten. Soy sauce is combined with a vegetable stock and added with ginger and garlic during kneading dough. Flavoring is limited only by your imagination. Then seitan is cooked in a combination of a vegetable stock and soy sauce.

Seitan and wheat gluten keep well in the freezer. in a sealed container or zip lock bag so make a larger batch and freeze for later, thawing for an hour or two first before using.

Seaweeds

Dry seaweed and pressed seaweed sheets known as "nori" can be soaked in water/broth to create a *fishy* flavor for vegetarian fish sausages.

Photo 2.22 Dry seaweed.

Photo 2.23 A sheet of nori.

Photo 2.24 A block of Nori looks like a rim of paper.

Photo 2.25 The sheets are fragile and can be cut or torn apart.

Legumes, Grains and Seeds

Grains are wonderful and nutritional fillers. They are very healthy with a high protein content and plenty of fiber which we do not eat enough, a well known fact. It may come as a surprise but the protein content of most grains equals that of lean meat. Seeds and nuts for example peanuts, soy beans and chick pea flour contain more protein than meat.

Grains are available as whole, cut or flour. You can use whole grains, however, the cooking process will be much shorter if they are cut into smaller parts. For example it is easier to work with steel cut oats than whole grains. Wheat comes as whole grain, steel cut and flour which comes in different varieties and colors. Smaller grains like buckwheat or millet are best used as whole. Certain grains are flattened, for example, rolled oats which we know as instant oats. For visual effects you may want whole grain wheat or rice in your recipe which is fine as long as you bind the ingredients properly so they stick together.

Name (The weight of grain=100 g)	Protein (g)	Fat (g)	Carbohydrates (g)	Fiber (g)	Calories
Amaranth, grain, uncooked	13.56	7.02	65.25	3.7	371
Barley, pearled, raw	9.91	1.16	77.72	15.6	352
Beans, black, raw	21.60	1.42	62.36	15.5	341
Beans, kidney, red, raw	22.53	1.06	61.29	15.2	337
Beans, white, raw	23.36	0. 85	60.27	15.2	333
Buckwheat	13.25	3.40	71.50	10.0	343
Chickpeas (Garbanzo)	20.47	6.04	62.95	12.2	378
Corn, fried, yellow	14.48	10.64	66.27	20.05	419
Flaxseed	28.88	42.16	28.88	27.3	534
Lentils, raw	24.63	1.06	63.35	10.07	352
Millet, raw	11.02	4.22	72.85	8.5	378
Oats, cereals, dry	13.15	6.52	67.70	10.1	379
Peas, green, split, raw	23.82	1.16	63.74	25.5	352
Poppy seed	17.99	41.56	28.13	19.5	525
Quinoa, uncooked	14.12	6.07	64.16	3.0	368
Rice, white, raw	6.50	0.52	79.15	2.8	358
Soybeans, raw	36.49	19.94	30.16	9.3	446
Sorghum grain	10.62	3.46	72.09	6.7	329
Teff, uncooked	13.30	2.38	73.13	8.0	367
Wheat, hard, white	11.31	1.71	75.90	12.2	342

Source: US National Nutrient Database
For more detailed analysis go to: http://ndb.nal.usda.gov/ndb/search

Poppy seeds are very small and are added whole to pastry products like bagels, however, for best results they should be ground with a seed grinder to release oil and flavor components. Whole poppy seeds are a familiar topping on a bagel, but ground poppy seeds are used in pastry, for example in Polish rolled cake known as "makowiec."

Photo 2.26 Poppy seeds.

Photo 2.27 Poppy seed roll.

Teff grass seeds originate in Ethiopia and are the smallest of all grains. Because of their size they are usually added whole. Teff seeds are great materials for snacks of the granola type.

Photo 2.28 Teff seeds.

Oats

Oats have numerous uses in foods; most commonly, they are rolled or crushed into oatmeal, or ground into fine oat flour. Oatmeal is chiefly eaten as porridge, but may also be used in baked goods. When cooked they develop a sticky gel which binds other ingredients.

Photo 2.30 Whole oats.

Photo 2.29 Whole oats, cut oats and rolled oats.

Whole grains are seldom used unless as feed for horses. Yes horses know good food and they absolutely love oats.

Steel cut oats are simply whole oat groats that have been cut into neat little pieces on a steel buhr mill which makes them faster to cook when making porridge. Also known as Irish oats or pinhead oats, steel cut oats create a chewy full-bodied hot cereal.

Photo 2.31 Cut oats.

Steel cut oats are the best choice for sausages as they develop a familiar chewy texture which feels like ground meat.

Instant oats are most popular as they are easy to prepare. They are called rolled oats because rotating steel drums flatten them out.

Photo 2.32 Rolled oats (instant).

Gums

You need starches, flours and gums to bind ingredients together, there is no way around it. Meat contains proteins which are released during cutting/grinding and these proteins dissolve in salt. As a result a sticky substance called *exudate* is created which binds meat particles together. Vegetarian sausages do not include meat or gelatin so we need more elaborate solutions to bind ingredients together, we need gums. Gums, technically referred to as hydrocolloids, originate from different sources. They can immobilize water and contribute viscosity. Two hydrocolloids that we are pretty familiar with are flour and starch, however, there are much stronger *natural* binders known as gums that are extracted from seaweeds and plants. If you look at processed food labels, you see all sorts of ingredients such as carrageenan, xanthan gum, konjac gum, locust bean gum, gum arabic, agar, and so on. The value of gums is not as a fat replacer but as a thickener which can combine with water and create gel. Gums fulfill several functions in food products:

1. They thicken things - ice cream, syrups, gravies, sauces.

2. They emulsify things - mixed liquids stay together without separating.

3. They change the texture - a gum will make something thicker.

4. They stabilize crystals - a gum might help prevent sugar or ice from crystallizing.

5. They help to reduce cooking loss which results in a higher yield and more succulent product.

The most popular gums are:

- Agar
- Alginate
- Carrageenan
- Gum Arabic
- Guar Gum
- Locust Bean Gum
- Konjac Gum
- Xantham Gum
- Pectin

While at first glimpse, such exotic names may discourage consumers from ever considering such products, the truth is that *they are natural products* which we consume all the time. The are added to ice creams, puddings, sauces and processed foods that require a creamy texture. Without gums sugar crystals will separate from ice cream and many products would turn into a watery mess.

We take for granted that manufactured foods should always look good and taste well, but there is more to that than meets the eye. Food products are made in one location, then stored in a different one and then transported many miles to a supermarket where they will sit on a shelf for some time. *Gums hold those products together.* Gums become more popular every day, some creative cooks design meals that are nothing short of magic, for example shrimp noodles or food pearls. Originally, only food technologists understood the subject, but today the gums are used in general cooking. Traditional jams were made by stirring a mixture of fruit and sugar for hours until it lost enough moisture to gel. Today *pectin* shortens the process to minutes and the product looks better and has a better consistency. Commercial producers need to use gums as their products, for example thinly sliced and packaged ham holds its shape together due to carrageenan gum. A hobbyist can also use less expensive things like gelatin, flour, eggs or protein concentrate, because the time between making the product and consumption is usually very short. Nevertheless, the information presented in this chapter will enable the reader to have a better understanding of the subject and will make it easier to further expand his knowledge by reading more technical books. What should make gums attractive to a vegetarian is that they are of vegetable origin as they are either made from seaweeds or from tubers or plants.

Agar - is made from the same family of red seaweeds as carrageenan. Agar is a natural *vegetable gelatin counterpart*. White and semi-translucent, it is sold in packages as washed and dried strips or in powdered form. Agar is approximately 80% fiber and is a very popular product in Asia. It can be used as an addition or as a replacement to pectin in jams and marmalades, as a substitute to gelatin for its superior gelling properties, and as a strengthening ingredient in souffles and custards. Agar is rather expensive.

Alginate - alginic acid, also called algin or alginate, is an anionic polysaccharide distributed widely in the cell walls of brown algae, where through binding water forms a viscous gum. In extracted form it absorbs water quickly; *it is capable of absorbing 200-300 times its own weight in water.* The chemical compound sodium alginate is the sodium salt of alginic acid. Sodium alginate is a flavorless gum used to increase viscosity and to act as an emulsifier.

Carrageenan is a natural extract from red seaweeds used in processed foods for stabilization, thickening, and gelation. During the heating process carrageenan can absorb plenty of water and trap it inside. This results in a higher cooking yield and less purge during storage. About 0.01% (1 g per kg of meat) can increase the yield of the finished product up to 8%.

Usually up to 1.0% (10 g/kg) of carrageenan is added to processed meats. Carrageenan forms a solid gel during cooling and improves sliceability. It also makes removal of the casing easier. Many vegetarians use carrageenan in place of products like gelatin since it is 100% vegetarian. *Adding carrageenan results in a firmer texture and improved sliceability.* Carrageenan must be heated to 180° F (82° C) before it forms a gel. The gel remains stable when the sausage cools down. Carrageenan works well in the presence of milk protein so using it with non-fat dry milk produces good results. Adding more than 1.5% carrageenan may result in a tough gummy texture.

There are three types of carrageenan employed in the food industry:

- **Kappa** - meat products, very strong gel. It is currently the most used type of carrageenan in low fat sausages.
- Iota - meat products, medium strong gel.
- Lambda - sauces and dressings. Does not gel.

Kappa carrageenan gels better in the presence of alkali agents such as potassium chloride (KCL). Enough potassium chloride is usually added to the carrageenan blend to create a strong gel. Potassium chloride is the same salt that is added to Morton's Low Salt, at 50% level, thus the salt itself promotes the development of strong gel. In addition milk protein is a strong promoter of carrageenan gels. Adding caseinate (milk protein) or non-fat dry milk will assist in the development of strong carrageenan gel.

Kappa and Iota carrageenan are only partially cold water soluble and need to be heated for full activation. Lambda carrageenan is fully cold water soluble.

Gellan gum is a high molecular weight polysaccharide (i.e., complex sugar) gum produced as a fermentation product by a pure culture of the microbe *Sphingomonas elodea*. Gellan gum is a food additive that acts as a thickening or gelling agent and can produce gel textures in food products ranging from hard and brittle to fluid. Gellan is used in bakery fillings, confections, dairy products, dessert gels, frostings, glazes, jams and jellies, low-fat spreads, and other products.

Photo 2.33 Gellan gum.

Guar gum - made from the seeds of a plant that grows in India and Pakistan. When placed in contact with water, guar gum will gel even at low concentrations (1% to 2%). About 1 teaspoon of gum gels one cup of water. Guar gum has been used for centuries as a thickening agent for foods and pharmaceuticals.

The gum is relatively inexpensive and commonly available.

Photo 2.34 Guar gum.

Gum Arabic

Gum arabic also known as *acacia gum,* is the hardened sap of the Acacia senegal tree, which is found in arid climates from Senegal on the west coast of Africa all the way to Pakistan and India. It is a natural emulsifier, which means that it can keep together substances which normally would not mix well. Pharmaceutical companies use it to keep medicines from separating into their different ingredients, and a dab of gum arabic makes newspaper ink more cohesive and permanent. Coca-Cola uses gum arabic to keep the sugar from precipitating to the bottom of its sodas. Gum arabic is tasteless and edible. As a food additive it has been extensively tested and is considered to be one of the safest additives for human consumption. Gum arabic has many non-food uses as well. It is used in paints, inks, glues, printing, cosmetics, photography, incense cones, shoe polish, postage stamps, cigarette paper adhesive, and pyrotechnic operations. In beverages, gum arabic helps citrus and other oil-based flavors remain evenly suspended in water. Gum arabic can be completely dissolved in its own volume of water. It is used in confectionery, glazes and artificial whipped creams. Gum arabic keeps flavor oils and fats uniformly distributed, retards crystallization of sugar, thickens chewing gums and jellies, and gives soft candies a desirable mouthfeel. In cough drops and lozenges, gum arabic soothes irritated mucous membranes. Many dry-packaged products such as instant drinks, dessert mixes and soup bases use it to enhance the shelf life of flavors. The gum is used in soft drink syrups, chocolate candies, gummy candies, and marshmallows. Like gelatin and carrageenan, gum arabic can be used to bind food substances as well as to smoothen textures or to hold flavoring.

Locust bean gum - locust bean gum, also known as carob gum, carob bean gum, and carobin is a galactomannan vegetable gum extracted from the seeds of the Carob tree, mostly found in the Mediterranean. The taste of locust bean powder is similar to ground cocoa powder but it contains less fat and calories than cocoa. It is dispersible in either hot or cold water. Locust bean gum is used in food products, cosmetics and other products.

Note: guar gum and *locust bean gum* belong to a group of gums that are known as *Galactomannans.*

Both gums are excellent thickeners and are added to low fat products to bind water. They are used in sausages to soften the texture and to facilitate stuffing. The clear advantage of both gums is that they can hold water at high temperatures, for example during the baking process which results in a better product.

Konjac Gum

Konjac flour also called konjac gum or konjac glucomannan is produced from the konjac plant root and can form meltable or heat stable gels. Konjac flour is rich in soluble fiber but does not contain starch or sugar so it does not have calories. *It is also gluten free.* Its thickening power is *10 times greater than cornstarch.* Konjac has the highest water holding capacity of any soluble fiber - up to 100 times its own water weight. One part of glucomannan can absorb 50 parts of liquid. About one teaspoon of konjac flour can gel about one cup of liquid, which may be water, meat stock or vegetable broth. Konjac powder can be used as a thickener for smooth gravies, sauces, glazes, soups, stews and casseroles. Konjac interacts synergistically with carrageenan, xanthan gum, locust bean gum. Konjac interacts with most starches increasing viscosity and allowing improvement of texture.

As a gelling agent, konjac exhibits the unique ability to form thermo-reversible and thermo-irreversible gels under different conditions:

- Reversible gum - konjac mixed with xanthan gum.
- Non-reversible gum - when heated at a pH of 9-10.

With the addition of a mild alkali such as calcium hydroxide, Konjac will set to a strong, elastic and thermo-irreversible gel. This gel will remain stable even when heated to 212° F (100° C) and above. Due to the thermo-irreversible property of the konjac gum, it has become popular to make a great variety of foods such as konjac cake, konjac noodles, and *foods for vegetarians.* Konjac flour improves binding but makes the removal of the casing skin harder. Konjac flour mixes with cold water extremely well and gelatinizes easily. It provides a slippery, fatty sensation, which results in a better mouthfeel. Additionally, it facilitates mixing and stuffing. The texture it creates is not as firm as the one made with carrageenan. That is why it is often combined with carrageenan.

Preparing Konjac gel:

If konjac flour is added directly to food, *it may create lumps.* Konjac powder thickens slowly when mixed with cold water but quickly thickens when heated. Mix konjac flour with cold water or other liquid first, stirring often until fully dissolved. Then add to a hot liquid or food that is cooking. It has no taste of its own so it inherits the flavor of the product. If you have not used konjac powder as a thickening agent before, it is best to experiment with it by beginning with lesser amounts and adding as necessary until the desired consistency is reached. Konjac is usually added at 0.25-0.50%

Photo 2.35 Konjac gum.

Xanthan Gum

Xanthan gum is produced by *fermentation* of glucose, sucrose, or lactose. During fermentation a strain of bacteria (*Xanthomonas campestris*) turns sugar into a colorless slime called xanthan gum. Xanthan gum is most often found in salad dressings and sauces. It helps to prevent oil separation by stabilizing the emulsion although it is not an emulsifier.

Xanthan gum also helps suspend solid particles such as spices. Also used in frozen foods and beverages, xanthan gum helps create the pleasant texture in many ice creams. Along with guar gum and locust bean gum Xanthan gum is soluble in cold water but in order to eliminate lumps it should be well agitated. Xanthan gum does not gelatinize when used alone but it can form gel at any pH when used with konjac gum.

At a ratio of 3 (xanthan) : 2 (konjac) the strongest gel is obtained. The gel is thermo-reversible: it is in solid state at temperatures below 40° C (104° F) but it will be in a semi-solid or liquid state at temperatures of 50° C (122° F) or above. When the temperature drops back to the ambient temperature <40° C (<122° F), it will resume the solid state. The addition of 0.02-0.03% konjac to 1% xanthan gum will raise its viscosity by 2-3 times under heating.

Photo 2.36 Xantham gum.

49

Gum Blends

It is often desirable to use a combination of gums to create a synergistic effect. Synergy means that a combined effect of two or more ingredients is greater than it would be expected from the additive combination of each ingredient. In this case the viscosity or gel strength will be greater if the following combinations are created:

- Xantham gum with guar gum.
- Xantham gum with bean gum.
- Konjac with carrageenan.
- Konjac with xanthan.

The above combinations may be used at a one-to-one ratio with each other. The synergistic effect is also present when a gum is combined with starch.

- Konjac with starch.
- Carrageenan with starch.
- Guar gum with starch.

Photo 2.37 A blend of xantham and konjac gum at the 3:2 ratio.

Adding modified starch and gum to food produces a similar effect. However, modified starch is less expensive than gum. Adding starch to ground meat is a universally accepted method. On the other hand 1 part of gum will produce a similar effect as 10 parts of starch so the result balances out. Using gum is more crucial in fine products like yoghurt or pie filling where the change in flavor and mouthfeel is easy to notice. Synergistic results of combining different gums are based on liquid gels. Those combinations may behave differently when added to sausages. They will definitely bind water and create gels but they may exhibit a weaker synergistic effect. The gums most often used in processed meats are: *carrageenan, xanthan and konjac*.

Pectin

Anybody who has recently made jams or jellies at home is familiar with pectin. Powdered or liquid pectin can be found in every supermarket. In the past jellied products were made by manually stirring fruit pulp until enough moisture was removed in order for the product to gel. Today pectin is added and the cooking process is cut down to a minute. The cooking loss is smaller and the product has more natural color. Although pectin can easily be made at home from apples or citrus fruit, it needs a significant amount of sugar to produce a gel. This restricts its use to making sweet fillings, jams, ice cream and other spreadable products, but not sausages, which in most cases do not contain sugar. The average store-bought pectin is a '*high-methoxyl*' product that requires at least a 55% sugar concentration to gel properly.

Low methoxy amidated pectin is a modified pectin that requires only a calcium source to gel and is used for making sugar free jams and jellies. Low methoxy amidated pectin creates a thermoreversible gel. This type of pectin is calcium sensitive, it will gel without the use of sugar although the addition of sugar will not affect the gelling process. It is activated by monocalcium, which is a rock mineral calcium source. There is calcium in the pectin mix. Low-methoxyl pectin is commonly used in a large number of sugar-free products such as: aspic, jams, yogurts, jelled pies, jelled milk puddings and candies, and jello. *Low-methoxyl pectin does not require sugar and can be used with meat products.* In emulsified meat products such as sausages, pates and meat spreads, pectin enables fat reduction and by *adding carrageenan in edition to pectin* a superior texture may be obtained. Hydrating in water prior to mixing with the meat would be best - use 1 part pectin to 5 parts water.

Coloring Agents

- Paprika - orange
- Smoked paprika - dark red
- Saffron - yellow
- Turmeric - yellow (used in curry)
- Caramel - brown (burnt sugar)
- Anatto - yellow/orange
- Ketchup, tomato paste - red
- Beet root - red, burgundy

Food and Drug Approved Red 4 is a great red colorant, however, it is cochineal extract which is made from bugs so it it is an animal product and will not conform to the requirements of pure vegetarians. It is used in the manufacture of artificial flowers, paints, crimson ink, rouge, and other cosmetics and is routinely added to food products and certain brands of juice most notably those of the ruby-red variety. Sausages made with dark spices will appear darker, black pepper is more visible that the white, rice and tofu are lighter than potatoes, textured vegetable protein is yellow, lentil is green or red, buckwheat groats grey, split green pea is green and beans come in many shapes and colors.

Annatto is an orange-red condiment and food coloring derived from the seeds of the achiote tree *(Bixa orellana)*.

Photo 2.39 Whole annatto seeds resemble buckwheat grouts in size and shape.

Photo 2.38 Ground annatto.

51

The colorant is typically prepared by grinding the seeds to a powder or paste. Ground annatto can be found in a spice section in a supermarket. It is often used to impart a yellow or orange color to foods but sometimes also for its flavor and aroma which is a combination of pepper and nutmeg. Annatto is widely used in many processed food products such as cheeses, dairy spreads, butter and margarine, custards, cakes and other baked goods, potatoes, snack foods, breakfast cereals, smoked fish, sausages, and more.

Beet Root

Photo 2.41 Beet powder creates an instant soup when mixed with water. It is a great colorant.

Photo 2.40 Beets produce a dark burgundy color juice which becomes absolutely beautiful pink when mixed with cream or white protein emulsion, see Chapter 4.

Show Material

Making each sausage in the form of a hot dog can be considered very rudimentary sausage making. Anybody can throw a bunch of ingredients into a food processor and stuff the paste into a sausage casing.

Well how about making a large diameter white looking sausage with pistachios, cranberries, raisins or prunes inside. Textured vegetable protein are irregular soy protein nuggets which not only look attractive but possess the bite and flavor of meat pieces. Showpiece material stands out and makes the sausage looking pretty. Diced tofu stands out well against darker materials.

Photo 2.42 Black beans act as show material in this quinoa sausage.

Typical Usage Amounts of Common Additives

Name	Common amount
Soy protein concentrate	1-3%
Soy protein isolate	1-3%
Non-fat dry milk	1-3%
Milk caseinate	2%
Whey protein concentrate	1-3%
Whey protein isolate	1-3%
Agar	0.2-3.0%
Alginate	0.5-1%
Carrageenan-Kappa	0.02-1.5%
Konjac	0.25-0.50%
Xanthan	0.02-0.03%
Locust bean gum (LBG)	0.1-1.0%
Gellan	0.4-0.7
Guar gum	0.1-0.7%
Gum Arabic	10-90%
Low methoxy pectin (LM Pectin)	0.5-3.0%
Gelatin	0.5-2.0%
Textured vegetable protein (TVP)	0.1-15%
Starch	1-5%
Oil	1-5%
Monosodium glutamate	0.2-1.0%

Flavor Enhancers

MSG (monosodium glutamate) is a flavor enhancer that is produced by the fermentation of starch, sugar beets, sugar cane, or molasses. Although once stereotypically associated with foods in Chinese restaurants, it is now found in many common food items, particularly processed foods. MSG is commonly available in food stores.

Ribonucleotide is a much stronger flavor enhancer than MSG and is carried by commercial producers.

Liquid smoke can be added to vegetarian sausages to obtain a smoky flavor.

Sesame seeds, especially the oil carry a unique slightly smoky flavor.

Summary of Important Issues

- Finely cut fillers such as flours and starches are usually added dry.
- Coarse fillers such as bread crumbs, rusk, cereals and TVP are usually re-hydrated before adding them to a mix.
- Don't add salt to cooking water when preparing rice, potatoes, barley or making meat stock. Salt will be added during mixing ingredients.
- Soy protein concentrate (or isolate) binds water and retains moisture during cooking. The sausage will look plumper.
- Non-fat dry milk binds water well.
- White of an egg binds all ingredients well together, but gelatin is stronger.
- Using prepared protein emulsion produces not only better sausages but makes the process simpler and faster.
- Adding 1% of powdered gelatin greatly improves texture of sausages, however, gelatin is made from pork skins.

Coconut Milk

Coconut milk can be used in many recipes.

Ingredient (100 g serving)	Protein (g)	Fat (g)	Carbohydrates (g)	Salt (mg)	Energy (cal)
Canned coconut milk	2.02	21.33	2.81	13	197
Source: USDA Nutrient database					

Chapter 3

Power of Soy

Soybeans were cultivated in Asia about 3,000 years ago. Soy was first introduced to Europe in the early 18th century and to British colonies in North America in 1765, where it was first grown for hay. Benjamin Franklin wrote a letter in 1770 mentioning bringing soybeans home from England. Soybeans did not become an important crop outside of Asia until about 1910. Soy was introduced to Africa from China in the late 19th Century and is now widespread across the continent.

In America soy was considered an industrial product only and not used as a food prior to the 1920's. Traditional non-fermented food uses of soybeans include soy milk and from the latter tofu and tofu skin. Fermented foods include soy sauce, fermented bean paste, natto, and tempeh, among others. Originally, *soy protein concentrates and isolates were used by the meat industry to bind fat and water in meat applications and to increase protein content in lower grade sausages.* They were crudely refined and if added at above 5% amounts, they imparted a "beany" flavor to the finished product. As technology advanced soy products were refined further and exhibit a neutral flavor today.

In the past the soybean industry begged for acceptance but today soybean products can be found in every supermarket. Differently flavored soy milk and roasted soybeans lie next to almonds, walnuts and peanuts. Today soy proteins are considered not just a filler material, but a "good food" and are used by athletes in diet and muscle building drinks or as refreshing fruit smoothies.

Soybeans

Soybeans are considered to be a source of complete protein. A complete protein is one that contains significant amounts of all the essential amino acids that must be provided to the human body because of the body's inability to synthesize them. For this reason soy is a good source of protein amongst many others for vegetarians and vegans or for people who want to reduce the amount of meat they eat. They can replace meat with soy protein products without requiring major adjustments elsewhere in the diet. From the soybean many other products are obtained such as: soy flour, textured vegetable protein, soy oil, soy protein concentrate, soy protein isolate, soy yoghurt, soy milk and animal feed for farm raised fish, poultry and cattle.

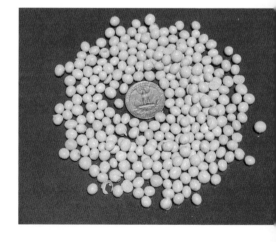

Photo 3.1 Soy beans.

Soybean Nutrient Values (100 g)					
Name	Protein (g)	Fat (g)	Carbohydrates (g)	Salt (g)	Energy (cal)
Soybean, raw	36.49	19.94	30.16	2	446

Soybean Fat Values (100 g)				
Name	Total Fat (g)	Saturated Fat (g)	Monounsaturated Fat (g)	Polyunsaturated Fat (g)
Soybean, raw	19.94	2.884	4.404	11.255
				Source: USDA Nutrient database

The dramatic increase in interest in soy products is largely credited to the 1995 ruling of the Food and Drug Administration allowing health claims for foods containing 6.25 g of protein per serving. The FDA approved soy as an official cholesterol-lowering food along with other heart and health benefits. The FDA granted the following health claim for soy: "25 grams of soy protein a day, as part of a diet low in saturated fat and cholesterol, may reduce the risk of heart disease."

Protein rich powders, 100 g serving					
Name	Protein (g)	Fat (g)	Carbohy-drates (g)	Salt (mg)	Energy (cal)
Soy flour, full fat, raw	34.54	20.65	35.19	13	436
Soy flour, low fat	45.51	8.90	34.93	9	375
Soy flour, defatted	47.01	1.22	38.37	20	330
Soy meal, defatted, raw, crude protein	49.20	2.39	35.89	3	337
Soy protein concentrate	58.13	0.46	30.91	3	331
Soy protein isolate, potas-sium type	80.69	0.53	10.22	50	338
Soy protein isolate (Su-pro®) *	92.50	2.8	0	1,400	378
					Source: USDA Nutrient database
* Data by www.nutrabio.com. Soy isolates sold by health products distributors online usually contain 92% of protein.					

Soy flour is made by milling soybeans. Depending on the amount of oil extracted the flour can be full-fat or de-fatted. It can be made as fine powder or more coarse soy grits. Protein content of different soy flours:

- Full-fat soy flour - 35%.
- Low-fat soy flour - 45%.
- Defatted soy flour - 47%.

Soy Proteins

Soybeans contain all three of the nutrients required for good nutrition: complete protein, carbohydrate and fat as well as vitamins and minerals including calcium, folic acid and iron. The composition of soy protein is nearly equivalent in quality to meat, milk and egg protein. Soybean oil is 61% polyunsaturated fat and 24% monounsaturated fat which is comparable to the total unsaturated fat content of other vegetable oils. Soybean oil contains no cholesterol.

Soy concentrates and isolates are used in sausages, burgers and other meat products. Soy proteins when mixed with ground meat *will form a gel* upon heating, entrapping liquid and moisture. They increase firmness and juiciness of the product and reduce cooking loss during frying. In addition they enrich the protein content of many products and make them healthier by reducing the amount of saturated fat and cholesterol that otherwise would be present. Soy protein powders are the most commonly added protein to meat products at around 2-3% as the larger amounts may impart a "beany" flavor to the product. They bind water extremely well and cover fat particles with fine emulsion. This prevents fats from lumping together. The sausage will be juicier, plumper and have less shrivelling.

Soy protein concentrate (about 60% protein), available from most online distributors of sausage making supplies is a *natural product* that contains around 60% protein and retains most of the soybean's dietary fiber. SPC can bind 4 parts of water. However, *soy concentrates do not form the real gel* as they contain some of the insoluble fiber that prevents gel formation; they only form a paste. This does not create a problem as the sausage batter will never be emulsified to the extent that the yoghurt or smoothie drinks are. Before processing, soy protein concentrate is re-hydrated at a ratio of 1:3.

Commercially processed meats contain soy protein today throughout the world. Soy proteins are used in hot dogs, other sausages, whole muscle foods, salamis, pepperoni pizza toppings, meat patties, vegetarian sausages etc. Hobbyist have also discovered that adding some soy protein concentrate allowed them to add more water and improved the texture of the sausage. It eliminated shrivelling and made the sausage plumper.

Soy protein isolate (80-90% protein), is a natural product that contains at least 80-90% protein and no other ingredients. It is made from de-fatted soy meal by removing most of the fats and carbohydrates. Therefore, soy protein isolate has a *very neutral flavour* compared to other soy products. As soy protein isolate is more refined, it costs slightly more than soy protein concentrate. Soy protein isolate can bind 5 parts of water. Soy isolates are excellent emulsifiers of fat and their *ability to produce the real gel* contributes to the increased firmness of the product. Isolates are added to add juiciness, cohesiveness, and viscosity to a variety of meat, seafood, and poultry products.

For making quality sausages the recommended mixing ratio is 1 part of soy protein isolate to 3.3 parts of water. SPI is chosen for delicate products that require superior flavor such as yoghurt, cheese, whole muscle foods and healthy drinks. Soy protein isolates sold by health products distributors online usually contain 92% of protein.

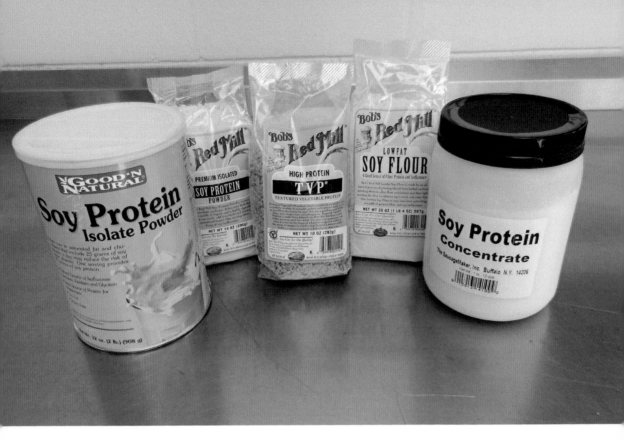

Photo 3.2 A variety of soy products.

Textured Vegetable Protein - TVP

Textured vegetable protein (TVP), also known as textured soy protein (TSP), soy meat, or soya meat has been around for more than 50 years. It contains 50% protein, little fat, no cholesterol and is very rich in fiber. It is an excellent relatively flavorless filler material for *vegetarian sausages*. Its protein content is equal to that of the meat, but TVP contains no fat.

TVP flakes are the size of finely ground meat and they have the texture and *the bite of the meat*. Textured vegetable protein is cheaper than meat and was used to extend meat value.

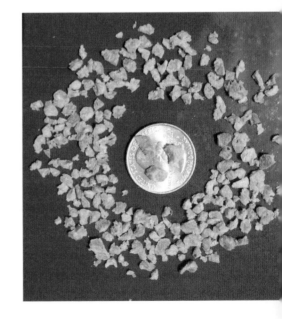

Photo 3.3 Textured vegetable protein (TVP) flakes and the quarter coin. TVP must be rehydrated with water/liquid before use.

Using TVP one can make vegetarian or vegan versions of traditionally meat-based dishes such as chili con carne, spaghetti bolognese, sloppy joes, tacos, burgers, or burritos.

Textured Vegetable Protein (100 g = 1 cup)					
Name	Protein (g)	Fat (g)	Carbohydrates (g)	Salt (mg)	Energy (cal)
TVP	50	0	30	8 mg	333
					Source: Bob's Red Mill

TVP flakes or powder are usually soaked in water (1 part of flakes to 2-3 parts of water) and then mixed with sausage materials to a ratio of up to 1:3 (rehydrated TVP to materials). TVP has no flavor of it's own and is practical to use as a meat substitute or extender. Besides, it offers the best value for the money. You may add up to 30% of TVP. TVP is a great ingredient for making *vegetarian foods*. TVP is made from high (50%) soy protein, soy flour or concentrate, but can also be made from cotton seeds, wheat and oats. It is extruded into various shapes (chunks, flakes, nuggets, grains, and strips) and sizes and is primarily used as a meat substitute due to its very low cost. When a TVP enriched meat product is cooked, it will lose less weight as TVP absorbs meat juices and water that would normally be lost.

The small granules of TVP are easy to rehydrate but hydration rates can further be improved by using warm water. However, the mixture must be cooled down before it can be blended with other materials. Rehydrated TVP must be refrigerated and treated like a meat. Usually 1 part of textured soy protein will absorb 2-3 parts of water. *TVP can be mixed with ground meat to a ratio of up to 1:3 (rehydrated TVP to meat)* without reducing the quality of the final product.

Textured soy flour (TSF) is obtained from regular soy flour which is processed and extruded to form products of specific texture and form, such as meat like nuggets. The formed products are crunchy in the dry form and upon hydration become moist and chewy.

Tofu

Tofu, also known as bean curd is a food made by coagulating soy milk and then pressing the resulting curds into soft white blocks. Tofu is a very nutritional product unfortunately it has a very bland flavor so it can be considered only a filler material, albeit a valuable one. However, its bland flavor can be compensated for by adding natural flavors such as apple, plum, strawberry, tomato, vegetable dry powders and spices.

Tofu (100 g)						
Name	Protein (g)	Fat (g)	Carbohydrates (g)	Salt (mg)	Energy (cal)	Cholesterol (mg)
Tofu, raw, regular	8.08	4.78	1.88	7	76	0
Tofu, raw, firm	15.78	8.72	4.27	14	145	0
						USDA Nutrient database

There are many different varieties of tofu including fresh tofu and tofu that has been processed in some way. Tofu is bought or made to be soft, firm, or extra firm. Tofu has a subtle flavor and can be used in savory and sweet dishes. It is often seasoned or marinated to suit the dish.

Photo 3.4 Tofu.

Photo 3.5 Dried soy been curd.

Tempeh

Tempeh is a traditional soy product originally from Indonesia. It is made by a natural culturing and controlled fermentation process. Like tofu, tempeh is made from soybeans but it is a whole soybean product which is *fermented*. The fermentation process and inclusion of whole soybeans result in a product with different texture and flavor. It is more difficult to create at home conditions so its suitability for making sausages is limited.

Photo 3.6 Tempeh.

Chapter 4

Emulsions

Why Do We Need Emulsion?

All sausages need fat. Fat carries flavor and provides a pleasant mouthfeel. Animal fat works great as it solidifies at room temperature. Melt animal fat, add finely chopped dry meat and berries to it and you will get the great Indian snack called Pemmican. It is rock hard and will last years without refrigeration. You cannot do it with oil.

Oil is liquid when heated and remains liquid when cold. You can add 50% of pork fat to the sausage and its texture will be fine. When more than 5% of vegetable oil is added to vegetarian sausage we get problems. The sausage is oily, soft and oil pockets appear. It gets under the skin of the casing and we get oily fingers trying to remove the casings.

We can hide oil inside of the emulsion and it will be neither seen nor sensed. The emulsion can hold a very large amount of oil. Take for example an egg emulsion, commonly known as mayonnaise. It is basically the yolk of an egg plus plenty of oil. Some salt, mustard, vinegar, this hardly counts at all. Yet this huge amount of oil looks pretty and tastes great.

The emulsion consists of emulsifier, fat (or oil) and water. We know that oil and water do not mix but they will in the presence of an emulsifier such as liver, yolk of an egg or a rich source of vegetable protein like soy protein isolate. Flaxseed is a great natural emulsifier.

Most food emulsions are known as the oil-in-water type, which means that oil (or fat) droplets are dispersed throughout the water. Put oil and water in a jar, shake it well and you'll disperse the oil. After a while the oil droplets will coalesce together and the layer of oil will be visible on top of the water. To disperse oil in water and prevent the oil droplets from coming together we need a substance known as an emulsifier.

Protein is needed to mix substances such as fat and water. Proteins are released from muscles during cutting or grinding. Salt and phosphates facilitate the release of proteins. Protein dissolves in salt and water and creates a liquid which coats each fat particle with a thin layer of soluble protein. Those coated fat particles combine with water and meat and the emulsion is created. The leaner the meat the more protein it contains. If little or no fat is used, there will not be any real emulsion and the proteins will simply hold the texture of the sausage together.

Vegetarian sausages do not contain meat so we use a material rich in protein such as soy protein isolate (90% protein) or flaxseed. The latter contains about 42% protein but is a wonderful emulsifier that produces quite a sticky emulsion.

Vegetable Protein Emulsions

Vegetarian sausages do not contain meat proteins, however, vegetable proteins produce stable emulsions, augment nutritional value of a sausage and eliminate cholesterol. The protein covers oil particles with a protein film and oil and water mix together becoming a true emulsion. Such emulsion looks, feels and tastes like fat, helps to achieve a better texture, provides plenty of protein and calories but none of the cholesterol. And it mixes well with all other ingredients.

Emulsifiers

Emulsifiers are essential in order to mix fat and water in foods. The principle ingredients of the emulsion are emulsifier, fat and water. The emulsifier contains proteins plus a significant amount of *mucilage* which is a mixture of gluey and gelatinous substances that form a matrix with fat particles and water droplets. Popular emulsifiers:

- meat protein
- milk protein (caseinate)
- egg yolk
- vegetable protein (soy protein or flaxseed)

Egg yolk contains many proteins that act as emulsifiers, the most important one *lecithin* prevents the surface of the fat droplet from coming into contact with the surface of another fat droplet. This is why egg yolks are so important in making foods such as hollandaise sauce and mayonnaise.

Sodium caseinate, a milk protein, is an excellent emulsifier that was commonly used to stabilize fat and water emulsions. Caseinate allowed to emulsify different types of fats from different animals. However, the price of milk proteins was increasing and soy proteins took over the dominant spot. Caseinate is about 90% protein and is added at 1-2% per kg of meat. Milk protein will lighten up the sausage and will make it slightly softer. It is added to meat batter as dry powder or as prepared emulsion. The emulsion is usually set at milk protein/fatty trimmings/water in the ratio of 1:5:5.

Note: Many vegetarians do not accept milk protein and egg yolk in their vegetarian diet.

Two emulsifiers of special interest for making vegetarian sausages are:

- soy protein
- flaxseed

If flaxseed or soy protein are mixed together with other ingredients in one step, the ingredients will separate. If flaxseed or soy protein emulsion is created first, then the emulsion will hold other ingredients together. If little or no fat is used, there will not be any real emulsion and the proteins will simply hold the texture of the sausage better.

Soy Protein Emulsion

Soy protein emulsion is easily made from soy protein **isolate**, vegetable oil and water. It has a consistency of a soft cream cheese, it is a white gel that looks and tastes like fat. Soy emulsion is easy and fast to make and can be stored in a refrigerator for up to 5 days.

soy protein isolate/oil/water 1 : 4 : 5	
SPI (92% protein)	10 g
Vegetable oil	40 g
Water	50 ml
Emulsion total:	100 g
Calories	398 cal

Soy protein isolate (SPI, 90% protein) produces the real emulsion gel: a white, soft, cream cheese-like substance that tastes like fat. Soy protein isolate is pure protein with a very few impurities and that is why it makes such a great emulsion.

SPI is water hungry so it is difficult to start emulsion with less than 5 parts of water. Once SPI and water are mixed into a paste 4 or more parts of oil can be added.

Photo 4.1 Soy protein isolate makes real smooth emulsion. Soy protein concentrate makes a high quality paste. Both powders have been used in meat sausages for many years. The Sausage Maker Inc has been distributing them for over 30 years.

Photo 4.2 Soy protein emulsion.

Making Emulsion

1. Using a food processor/blender or manual whisk start cutting cold water with *soy protein isolate* until a shiny paste is obtained. This takes about one minute.
2. Add chilled oil and cut at high speed until a stable emulsion is obtained. It should take about 2 minutes.
3. Store emulsion for up to 5 days in a refrigerator.

Photo 4.3 Protein emulsion.

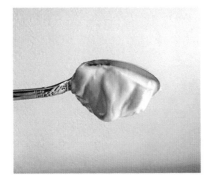

Photo 4.4 The emulsion sticks to the spoon.

Photo 4.5 The emulsion holds its shape even when heated for 10 min at 176° F (80° C).

Flaxseed

Flaxseed is a very nutritious and rich in fiber seed that is often used as an emulsifier in the baking industry.

Flaxseed Nutrient Values (100 g)					
Name	Protein (g)	Fat (g)	Carbohydrates (g)	Cholesterol (g)	Energy (cal)
Flaxseed	18.29	42.16	28.88	0	534
				Source: USDA Nutrient database	

Flaxseed has a sufficient amount of gelatinous substances for forming suitable emulsions.

The following ratios will produce suitable emulsions:

- flaxseed, 3-10%
- vegetable oil, 60-80%
- water, 10-30%

The fat can be of animal or vegetable nature; corn, sunflower or olive oil is suitable.

Making Flaxseed Emulsion (1:3:3)

10 g ground flaxseed : 30 ml water : 30 ml oil

Flaxseed must be milled to the smallest particle possible. The labor consuming process of grinding seeds can be eliminated by buying milled seeds in a supermarket.

Photo 4.6 Ground flaxseed on the right.

Photo 4.7 Milled flaxseed by Bob's Red Mill
www.bobsredmill.com

Blend milled flaxseed with water on medium speed until a paste is obtained. Start adding oil and blend all together on high speed. Blend until a uniform texture is obtained without any pockets of oil, water or flax.

Photo 4.8 Blending milled seeds with water and oil. You need to make at least 100 g (3.5 oz) of emulsion in order to cover the knife of the blender.

Photo 4.9 Flax seed emulsion. Store emulsion in a refrigerator. The flaxseed emulsion is sticky. It is greyish in color due to miniscule parts of seed with a certain flavor of its own. Very good with grains.

Soy protein emulsion is almost neutral in flavor, very smooth and white in color. Best for creamy texture sausages where the uniform color is desired.

Emulsions can be made with **milk caseinate** or **whey protein**, however, these proteins do not meet vegan standards. Whey protein is made by drying liquid whey which is a byproduct obtained during cheese making. Similarly to soy products whey protein comes as:

- Whey protein concentrate, 30-89% protein.
- Whey protein isolate, 90% or more.

Whey is essential in the bodybuilding world today because of its ability to be digested very rapidly.

The following two emulsions work very well in vegetarian sausages:

Emulsion	Protein	Oil	Water
Soy protein (100 g)	10 g	40 g	50 g
Flaxseed (50 g)	10 g	20 g	20 g
Flaxseed (100 g)	20 g	40 g	40 g

Better Emulsion

The secret for making high quality emulsion is very simple: *replace water* which has no taste with a liquid of your choice such as vegetable broth or juice. The resulting emulsion will have a different flavor and color.

Photo 4.10 Soy emulsion.

Photo 4.11 Flaxseed emulsion. A very strong elastic emulsion with oat porridge like feel.

Photo 4.12 Red soy emulsion. Water replaced with beet juice. Wonderful flavor.

Photo 4.13 Soy emulsion. Water replaced with beet juice. White horseradish sauce added.

Photo 4.14 Soy emulsion with water which was colored with saffron spice.

Photo 4.15 Soy emulsion with added annatto powder.

67

You can make your own broth by boiling soup greens or buy ready to use commercially made vegetable broth which may even be flavored, for example vegetarian beef broth. The simplest solution is to use vegetarian bouillon cubes.

Soy Emulsion With Soy Sauce

Adding soy sauce to soy emulsion produces a unique miso like flavored product. Miso is a traditional Japanese thick paste produced by fermenting soybeans with salt and the fungus. Miso is used for sausces and spreads, pickling vegetables or meats, and making miso soup, a Japanese culinary staple.

10 g soy protein isolate
40 ml oil
20 ml soy sauce mixed with 30 ml of water

Do not increase the amount of soy sauce. The emulsion can be combined with seaweeds like *nori* to make a vegetarian fish sausage.

Photo 4.16 Soy emulsion with soy sauce.

Customized emulsions can be designed to suit a particular application. For example replacing water with tomato juice creates soy protein tomato emulsion.

Photo 4.17 Soy protein emulsion with coconut milk.
1 part protein : 4 parts oil : 7 parts coconut milk.

Photo 4.18 Soy protein emulsion with tomato juice.
1 part soy protein isolate : 4 parts oil : 5 parts tomato juice.

Flaxseed coconut emulsion can be made with 1 part ground flaxseed and 7 parts of coconut milk without additional oil needed.

Soy Protein Paste

Soy protein concentrate (SPC, 70% protein) is commonly added to home made meat sausages, but will not produce an emulsion, just a paste *which looks like emulsion*. It is not as smooth as emulsion, it is somewhat grainy so you will not use it in applications like ice cream or fine yogurt. It is perfectly acceptable for making sausages of any kind. SPC needs only 3 parts of water, the amount of oil can vary from 2 parts to more.

A typical SPC paste (1:3:3):
10 g SPC : 30 ml oil :30 ml water.

Vegan Mayonnaise

By now you might have discovered that a soy emulsion is basically a vegan mayonnaise, all you need to add is some salt, vinegar and mustard powder (or prepared mustard). Expensive vegan mayonnaise is nothing else than spiced up protein emulsion that you can make yourself.

There are many ways to make eggless mayonnaise. Most recipes call for blending whole milk and lemon juice. As milk does not really conform to vegan requirements so other recipes include *soy milk,* oil, lemon juice and seasonings which are better.

Soy Protein Mayonnaise

Soy protein isolate, 20 g
Water, 100 ml
Oil, 125 ml
Salt,
Lemon juice, 2 tsp
Preapared mustard, 1 tsp

Blend SPI with water and lemon juice.
Gradually add oil and blend together.
Add salt, mustard and seasonings of your choice and blend together.

Photo 4.19 Due to its neutral flavor soy protein isolate will not influence the flavor of the mayonnaise.

Soy Milk Vegan Mayonnaise

Soy milk makes wonderful, white and easy to produce mayonnaise. Taste soy milk first as even traditional original soy milk made by different manufacturers exhibits different flavors. Some milk tastes beany while other is sweet, those flavors may be present in a finished product.

Soy milk, 120 ml (1/2 cup)
Canola oil, 250 ml (1 cup)
Lemon juice, 2 tsp
Pinch of salt
Prepared mustard, 1 tsp

Blend soy milk with lemon juice.
Add oil and blend.
Add salt and mustard and blend all together.

Photo 4.20 Soy milk mayonnaise.

Add ketchup and you will create Russian dressing which may become a part of a vegetarian tomato sausage. Add ketchup and creamy horseradish sauce and you will create cocktail sauce.

Emulsions and mayonnaise can be very useful for making sausages. The main benefit they offer in making vegetarian sausages is their ability of binding and holding the oil inside.

Note: all emulsion ratios are by weight, for example soy protein emulsion (1:4:5) is made by blending 10 g soy protein with 40 g oil and 50 g water. Protein is mixed with water first and then oil is added.

Chapter 5

Recipes

Recipe Guidelines

The recipes are strictly vegan. You can add at your discretion, an egg, non-fat dry milk and that will only improve the texture of the sausage. Gelatin is a wonderful binder, however, it is made from animal skins and bones. There are dozens of natural animal or collagen casings of different diameter but they are of animal origin and are not included in recipes.

Modifying Meat Sausage Recipes

Vegetarian sausages can be made from countless combinations of fillers and spices. Take blood sausages for example. Except 10-20% of blood and occasional addition of meat, the sausages are made with buckwheat, barley, rice, rusk or bread crumbs. Replace blood with flax emulsion and you will end up with a vegetarian sausage. Remove meat from Swedish potato sausage and replace with textured vegetable protein, however, keep potatoes and the same spices. There are many known meat sausages that include filler material such as potatoes, bread crumbs, oats, buckwheat and barley groats, semolina and potato flour, rusk, cracker meal and rice. Remove the meat component from the recipes, replace with a suitable vegetarian equivalent, leave the original spices and you will create a vegetarian version of a well known recipe. Just make sure the ingredients don' fall apart when the sausage is sliced. Generally, it can be assumed that if a particular material for example semolina flour was added to meat sausage, it should make a good vegetarian sausage as well.

Cooking Sausages

The majority of meat sausages are cooked in water. This method produces the best results for vegetarian sausages as well. Cooking distributes ingredients better and is necessary to activate carrageenan, which gelatinizes at around 180° F (82° C). Potato starch gelatinizes at lower temperatures, nevertheless it also must be heated. It can be easily noticed that a sausage that feels soft after stuffing will firm up after only a few minutes of heat treatment. The grains and the flour are safe at room temperature only because they do not contain moisture. The moisture is introduced during mixing ingredients as they are usually precooked or soaked in water. This is an invitation to bacteria which they will definitely accept and the spoilage begins. Cooking stuffed sausage kills bacteria and slows down the spoilage. After stuffing the sausage may be placed in a refrigerator or frozen, however, they have to be cooked before serving which sets the additives and makes the sausage firmer. It is a good idea to immerse cooked sausages for 5 minutes in cold water. This step diminishes shriveling of the casing. The freshly stuffed uncooked sausage has a very limited shelf life and its texture is poor, once it is cut it will keep losing moisture and its texture will improve.

Moisture Control

The manufacture of vegetarian sausages presents certain problems. The amount of salt or spices you can always adjust, however, if the texture of the sausages is soft, it will be soft every time. Fillers such as grains or beans do absorb water during soaking and cooking, however, they don't stick together. They are don't have "meat glue" that ground meat develops when mixed with salt. It is easy to cook grains in sufficient amounts of water so they become sticky and will not separate, however, when stuffed the sausage will become very soft. We could draw out the excess of water by adding gums which will convert water into a gel. This, however, is of a little help as the gel is soft as well. Gums work wonderfully with jellies and sauces which have a soft texture but the sausages must be firmer. Make sure you don't add too much water to grains when cooking. If they are too soft let them steam at low heat until more moisture evaporates.

Take note that materials such as bread crumbs, cracker meal, textured vegetable protein (TVP) and rusk are usually rehydrated 2-3 times their weight in water. Raisins, dry fruit and flour will absorb water as well. If you want to use a significant amount of soft moist material for example tofu, mix it with water hungry fillers like TVP, bread crumbs or cracker meal but in their original *dry* form. They will absorb water from tofu and the resulting mixture will be much firmer. Both soy protein concentrate and isolate will draw water as well. The advice is to add such ingredients that will not only draw out water but will act as a filler increasing the weight of the sausage. Potato flour is such a filler. If you end up with a soft stuffing mix, add some flour. Vital wheat gluten is an excellent thickener and filler, however, some people are allergic to it so we have tried to limit its use in recipes. *You don't need tofu in every recipe.* It will make all your sausages very similar besides all types of tofu are soft. However, when added at 10-20%, it makes a great show material. If you want to add more tofu, combine it with a dry filler that absorbs water such as bread crumbs, TVP, dry raisins, cranberries or others. Those dry fillers will draw water out of tofu making the mixture much firmer. Once when the sausage is cut its texture will start to harden due to evaporation of moisture. The texture will be very firm in a day or two.

Any food cooked at home can be enriched with starch, flour, or gum, stuffed into a casing and made into a sausage.

Oil

Oil presents another problem. It is needed to provide a better mouthfeel, unfortunately it is a liquid and a slippery one. It is soft and finds its own path to flow which might result in oil pockets. Gums will not bind oil. When flour or starch is heated in oil it will produce a thickening paste known as "roux" which then thickens soups, sauces or gravies. This is general cooking which is technical, time consuming and of no practical use in the sausage making process. *The best way to immobilize oil is to hide it inside an emulsion.* A good example is mayonnaise; it looks appealing, tastes good, and includes plenty of oil which is hidden inside. Oil disappears inside of the emulsion, will not leak, yet still produces a good "mouthfeel." The emulsion hides and locks the oil away but it remains soft so you have to be careful about how much is added. If you mix oil *directly* with ingredients limit the amount of oil to around 3% otherwise the sausage might become oily. Up to 8% of oil can easily be added to emulsion but it is recommended to use emulsion at 5-20% otherwise a soft sausage will be produced. A good idea is to mix oil with flour or soy protein which creates a paste.

Stuffing

Stuff hard, this is the best advice. Synthetic casings are extremely strong. Do not remove air pockets with a needle as flour, starch or gum will leak out during cooking.

Manipulating Recipes

After a while, you will "feel" the recipe and be able to modify it at will. Follow the two examples below.

I. *Soaked* bread crumbs, 600 g (200 g dry bread crumbs soaked in 400 ml of water)
Tofu, 200 g
Flaxseed emulsion, 50 g
Potato flour, 50 g
Potato starch, 25 g
Guar gum, 10 g
Carrageenan, 10 g
Spices

Let's now assume that you want to triple the amount of tofu in the recipe. Well, the sausage texture will be too soft as tofu will introduce plenty of water. The solution will be to add dry bread crumbs or cracker meal as they will draw water out of tofu.

II. Smashed tofu, 600 g
Dry bread crumbs, 200 g
Flaxseed emulsion, 50 g
Potato flour, 50 g
Potato starch, 25 g
Guar gum, 10 g
Carrageenan, 10 g
Spices

Tofu is smashed or diced finely to facilitate removal of water by bread crumbs.

Think Metric

It is recommended that the sum of all ingredients in a recipe comes to 1000 g as close as possible. This is how professional recipes are designed. For home sausage making 950 g total is acceptable. This makes all calculations incredibly easy, for example in our recipe above 50 g of potato flour is 5%, guar gum equals 1% and 200 g of tofu is 20%. All professional recipes are written that way although meat plants make bigger batches of product where one unit equals 100 kg (220 lbs) which is 100%. If 2% of spice is needed, this comes to 2 kg. There is no need for a calculator when using metric.

A typical recipe that will work with most grains or legumes:

Dominant grain, 500 g
Secondary fillers-beans, tofu, 300 g
Flaxseed emulsion (1:2:2), 100 g
Potato starch, 25 g
Guar gum, 10 g
Carrageenan, 10 g
Spices

The **potato starch-guar gum-carrageenan** combination binds different ingredients very well. This combination works synergically, this means that its combined effect is greater than the sum that its individual components could provide.

Emulsions

The basic ratio for flaxseed emulsion is 1:2:2, 10 g flaxseed : 20 g oil : 20 g water, the total of 50 g. Most recipes call for 100 g emulsion. When added in the amount of 100 g to 1 kg of total material, 20 g flaxseed : 40 ml oil : 40 ml water, the emulsion provides 2% flaxseed, 4% oil and 4% of water.

Ground flaxseed mixed with 2-3 parts of water (no additional oil needed), creates a sticky paste which is a good substitute for an egg.

Soy protein emulsion (1:4:5) is very smooth without any visible particles, it has a very uniform color and a pleasant flavor. It is a good choice for sausages of uniform color such as hot dogs. When added at 100 g to 1 kg of total material, 10 g soy protein : 40 g oil : 50 ml water, the emulsion provides 1% protein, 4% oil and 5% water.

To sum it up both emulsions are very similar, the flaxseed emulsion introduces a little less water, is darker with minute particles of seeds visible and it has a certain individual flavor. It is somewhat sticky what makes it particularly attractive for binding purposes and is a great choice for grains. Additionally, flaxseed contributes to a better digestion.

Spices

Go easy on salt, vegan sausage needs less salt than meat sausage. Be generous with spices, vegan sausage needs more spices than meat sausage.

Using Measuring Cylinder

You don't need to weigh water, vegetable stock, juice or soy sauce. Each 1 ml of water weighs exactly 1 g. Let's say you need 50 g of water. Just fill the cylinder to 50 ml mark and you have measured 50 g of water.

Oil weighs slightly less than an equivalent volume of water, for example 1 tablespoon of water weighs 15 g and 1 tablespoon of oil weighs 14 g. There will be, however, a very minor error if we assume them to be equal and use the measuring cylinder.

1 oz = 28.35 g
1 oz fluid = 30 ml
1 ml of water = 1 g
1000 ml of water = 1 liter = 1000 g = 1 kg (2.2 lb)
1 Tbsp = 3 tsp

Photo 5.1 Carrageenan contributes to better peelability.

Replacing Water with Vegetable Stock

Best blood sausages are produced when barley or buckwheat groats are cooked in leftover meat stock that was obtained from boiling meats and bones. The groats absorb the meat stock flavor and a superior quality product is obtained. The same technique can be applied to vegetarian sausages if a vegetable stock is used instead of water. Vegetarian sausages incorporate plenty of filler material such as grains or beans. Emulsions need water, wheat gluten is made by mixing flour with water.

The flavor of the sausages will greatly improve if *a vegetable stock is used instead of water.* The stock can be prepared by boiling soup greens or dissolving commercially produced *vegetable* bouillon cubes in water. Some filler material such as rice, grains or groats can be boiled in a vegetable stock, other material like beans, dry rolls, or textured vegetable protein (TVP) can be soaked in stock.

Photo 5.2 Vegetable bouillon cubes made by Knorr®.

Photo 5.3 Homemade broth from soup greens.

Photo 5.4 Left-homemade broth, right- broth made from bouillon cubes.

It is doubtful that all of us will suddenly start cooking vegetable stock if only for the lack of space in the refrigerator or freezer. On the other hand, how hard is it to throw a bouillon cube into boiling water.

Eat Them Cold

Most sausages are eaten cold. Yes we grill and boil some sausages and although they may be consumed in the USA in large quantities, nevertheless the fact remains that most sausages in the world are eaten cold. Use your own judgement, you will probably heat up Potato Sausage, but eat cold Granola or Polenta with Cranberries.

Recipe Index

Barley Red Sausage

Barley was one of the first cultivated grains and is now grown widely. When fermented, barley is used as an ingredient in beer and other alcoholic beverages. It is used in soups and stews, and as a filler material in blood sausages.

Photo 5.5 Barley sausage.

Cooked barley, 650 g (1.43 lb)
Soy-beet emulsion (1:4:5)* 100 g (3.5 oz)
TVP, 30 g (1 oz)
Beet juice for TVP, 90 ml (3 oz fl)
Vital wheat gluten, 50 g (1.76 oz)
Potato starch, 15 g (0.52 oz)
Guar gum, 5 g (0.17 oz)
Carrageenan, 10 g (0.35 oz)
Salt, 5 g (0.17 oz)
Pepper, 4 g (0.14 oz)
Onion powder, 10 g (0.35 oz)
Marjoram, 2 g (0.07 oz)
Oregano, 2 g (0.07 oz)
Allspice, 2 g (0.07 oz)

Cook barley in water for about 20 minutes. Use 1 part barley to 2.1 parts of water.

* make standard emulsion using beet juice instead of water.

Rehydrate TVP in beet juice instead of water.

Vital wheat gluten flour may be replaced with potato flour.

Mix barley, soy-beet emulsion, soaked TVP with spices together. Lastly, add starch, guar and carrageenan and mix all together.
Stuff hard into 38 mm casing.
Cook in 176-185° F (80-85° C) water for 20 minutes. Place sausages in cold water for 5 minutes. Remove and let them cool.

Basic Sausage

Wheat gluten, 750 g (1.65 lb)
Flaxseed emulsion (1:2:2), 200 g (7 oz)
Potato starch, 20 g (0.7 oz)
Guar gum, 10 g (0.35 oz)
Carrageenan, 10 g (0.35 oz)
Salt, 12 g (0.42 oz)
Pepper, 2 g (0.07 oz)
Garlic, 5 g (0.17 oz)

Photo 5.6 Basic Sausage.

Mix ground gluten with flaxseed emulsion and spices. Add starch, guar and carrageenan and mix all together.
Stuff hard into 38 mm casing.
Cook in 176-185° F (80-85° C) water for 20 minutes. Place sausages in cold water for 5 minutes. Remove and let them cool.

Bean Sausage

Cooked beans, 500 g (1.10 lb)
Wheat gluten, 250 g (0.55 lb)
Potato flour, 60 g (2.11 oz)
Soy emulsion (1:4:5), 100 g
Potato starch, 25 g (0.88 oz)
Guar gum, 10 g (0.35 oz)
Carrageenan, 10 g (0.35 oz)
Salt, 12 g (0.42 oz)
Pepper, 2 g (0.07 oz)
Paprika, 4 g (0.14 oz)
Onion powder, 5 g (0.17 oz)
Cumin, 4 g (0.14 oz)
Cayenne, 0.5 g (0.01 oz)
Water as needed, 100 ml (3.5 oz)

Photo 5.7 Bean sausage.

Soak beans in water for 4 hours. Drain, then slow cook until tender. Use enough water to cover the beans. You can use canned beans, just wash and drain them. Take a masher and mash them.
Add beans, chopped or ground wheat gluten, soy emulsion, spices and 100 ml water into food processor and chop until a paste is obtained. Add starch, guar gum and carrageenan and emulsify.
Add potato flour and emulsify.
Stuff hard into 38 mm casings.
Cook in 176-185° F (80-85° C) water for 20 minutes. Place sausages in cold water for 5 minutes. Remove and let them cool.

Beet - Horseradish with Tofu

Beet and horseradish is often served with meats and sausages. It also makes an interesting and tasty sausage.

Beets, cooked and grated, 500 g (1.1 lb)
Horseradish, grated, 100 g (3.5 oz)
Tofu, 200 g (7 oz)
SPI, 25 g (0.88 oz)
Potato flour, 60 g (2.1 oz)
Lemon juice, 15 ml (0.52 oz)
Sugar, 25 g (0.88 oz)
Salt, 10 g (0.35 oz)
Pepper, 2 g (0.07 oz)
Cinnamon, 1 g (0.03 oz)

Potato starch, 25 g (0.88 oz)
Guar gum, 10 g (0.35 oz)
Carrageenan, 10 g (0.35 oz)

Photo 5.8 Beet-Horderadish Sausage.

Slow cook whole beets until soft. Peel the skin, it slides off easily. Using a grater grate the beets. Grate horseradish. Dice tofu into 1/4" cubes.
Mix beets, horseradish, tofu, SPI, lemon juice, sugar and spices together. Mix the mass with starch, guar and carrageenan and mix. Add potato flour and mix all together.
Stuff hard into 38 mm casings. Cook in 176-185° F (80-85° C) water for 20 minutes.
Place sausages in cold water for 5 minutes. Remove and let them cool.

Bread Crumbs Sausage

A basic sausage that can be served cold or hot.

Plain bread crumbs, 250 g (0.55 lb)
Water, 400 ml (13.3 oz fl)
Soy emulsion (1:4:5), 200 g (7 oz)
Vital wheat gluten flour*, 50 g (1.76 oz)
Potato starch, 10 g (0.35 oz)
Guar gum, 10 g (0.35 oz)
Carrageenan, 10 g (0.35 oz)
Salt, 5 g (0.17 oz)
White pepper, 2 g (0.07 oz)
Allspice, 1 g (0.03 oz)
Onion powder, 10 g (0.35 oz)
Chopped parsley, 2 tablespoons

Photo 5.9 Bread Crumbs Sausage.

Soak bread crumbs for 20 minutes in 400 ml of water.
Mix bread crumbs, soy emulsion and spices together. Add starch, guar, carrageenan and vital wheat gluten flour and mix all together.
Stuff hard into 38 fibrous casings. Cook in 176-185° F (80-85° C) water for 20 minutes.
Place sausages in cold water for 5 minutes. Remove and let them cool.

* People allergic to gluten may replace vital wheat gluten flour with potato flour.

Bread Pudding Sausage

Bread pudding is eaten all over the world. It is made from white wheat bread or rolls, with milk, eggs, sugar and flavorings such as honey, raisins and vanilla. Milk has been replaced with coconut milk, honey may be replaced with maple syrup. Bread pudding is baked in oven, however, boiling sausage in water delivers a great product.

Photo 5.10a Bread Pudding Sausage.

White bread, 500 g (1.10 lb)
Soy-coconut emulsion (1:4:7), 240 g (0.52 lb). Blend 20 g of soy protein isolate with 140 ml (4.6 oz fl) coconut milk) and 80 ml oil.
Raisins, 50 g (1.76 oz)
Crushed walnuts, 50 g (1.76 oz)
Honey (maple syrup), 50 g (1.76 oz)
Sugar, 60 g (2.11 oz)
Potato starch, 25 g (0.88 oz)
Guar gum, 10 g (0.35 oz)
Carrageenan, 10 g (0.35 oz)
Vanilla extract, 50 ml (1.66 oz fl)

Photo 5.10b Bread Pudding Sausage.

Crumble white bread into smaller pieces. Combine bread and soy coconut emulsion. Add raisins, walnuts, honey, sugar, vanilla extract and mix together. Add starch, guar, carrageenan and mix all together.
Stuff hard into 38 mm casings.
Cook in 176-185° F (80-85° C) water for 20 minutes. Place sausages in cold water for 5 minutes. Remove and let them cool.

Photo 5.10c Bread Pudding Sausage.

Buckwheat Sausage

Triangular buckwheat groats are commonly used in western Asia and eastern Europe. Porridge was common, and was often considered the definitive peasant dish. The dish was brought to America by Ukrainian, Russian and Polish immigrants who called it kasha and they used it as a filling for cabbage rolls, knishes or served with meats and goulash. Buckwheat is a popular ingredient in blood sausages.

Buckwheat is a short season crop that grows well on poor-fertility or acidic soil. Unlike other crops, buckwheat responds negatively to too much fertilizer, especially nitrogen. Once we discovered fertilizers other grains became more profitable as they responded well to fertilizers. Buckwheat contains no gluten.

Cooked buckwheat groats, 500 g (1.1 lb)
Flaxseed emulsion (1:2:2), 200 g (7 oz)
Tofu, 150 g (5.3 oz)
Potato flour, 50 g (1.76 oz)
Guar gum, 10 g (0.35 oz)
Carrageenan, 10 g (0.35 oz)
Salt, 5 g (0.17 oz)
Pepper, 4 g (0.14 oz)
Allspice, 1 g (0.03 oz)
Cayenne pepper, 0.5 g (0.01 oz)
Onion powder, 15 g (0.52 oz)

Photo 5.11a Buckwheat Sausage.

Buckwheat to water ratio 1:1.8

Measure 200 g buckwheat and 450 ml of water. Bring water to a boil, add buckwheat and simmer partially covered for 15 minutes. Do not stir. Switch off the heat and leave groats uncovered to cool for 30 minutes. Make flaxseed emulsion (1:2:2). Dice tofu and mix with all ingredients except (0.5 oz fl) potato flour, guar gum and carrageenan. Add carrageenan, guar gum and potato flour and mix all together. Stuff hard into 38 mm casings without delay.
Cook in 176-185° F (80-85° C) water for 20 minutes. Place sausages in cold water for 5 minutes. Remove and let them cool.

Photo 5.11b Buckwheat Sausage.

Cajun

Wild rice, boiled, 600 g (1.32 lb)
Vital wheat gluten flour, 80 g (2.82 oz)
Soy protein emulsion (1:4:5), 100 g (3.5 oz)
Soy protein isolate, 20 g (0.7 oz)
Potato starch, 10 g (0.35 oz)
Guar gum, 10 g (0.35 oz)
Carrageenan, 10 g (0.35 oz)
Onion, chopped, 50 g (1.76 oz)
Celery, finely chopped, 50 g (1.76 oz)
Red bell pepper, chopped, 50 g (1.76 oz)
Jalapeno pepper, chopped, 30 g (1.5 oz)
Parsley, finely chopped, 20 g (2 Tbsp)
Salt, 15 g (0.52 oz)
Cracked black pepper, 6.0 g (0.21 oz)
Dried thyme, 2.0 g (0.07 oz)
½ bay leaf, crushed
Hot sauce, 15 ml (0.5 oz fl)
Water as needed, about 100 ml (3.3 oz fl)

For 1 volume part of wild rice use
2 parts of water. Wild rice needs more
cooking time, around 40-50 minutes.
Use a mild hot sauce, for example
Mexican Cholula Hot sauce. Vital wheat
flour may be substituted with potato
flour.

Photo 5.12a Cajun Sausage.

Photo 5.12b Cajun Sausage.

Save vital wheat gluten flour, starch, guar and carrageenan. Mix rice, soy emulsion, soy
protein isolate with all diced vegetables and spices.
Add starch, guar, carrageenan and vital wheat gluten flour and mix all together. Add
water as needed.
Stuff hard into 38 mm casings.
Cook in 176-185° F (80-85° C) water for 20 minutes. Place sausages in cold water for 5
minutes. Remove and let them cool.

Chorizo

Wheat gluten, 800 g (1.76 lb)
Soy protein isolate, 30 g (1.05 oz)
Soy emulsion, 100 g (3.5 oz)
Vital wheat gluten flour, 60 g (2.1 oz)
Guar gum, 10 g (0.35 oz)
Carrageenan, 10 g (0.35 oz)
Salt, 12 g (0.35 oz)
Pepper, 2 g (0.07 oz)
Smoked paprika (pimentón), 8 g (0.28 oz)
Oregano, rubbed, 2 g (0.07 oz)
Cayenne pepper, 0.5 g (0.01 oz)
Garlic, 7 g (2 cloves) (0.28 oz)

Photo 5.13 Chorizo.

Grind wheat gluten through a small plate.
Except gluten flour, guar and carrageenan, mix all ingredients together. Add gluten flour, guar and carrageenan and mix all together.
Stuff hard into 38 mm casings.
Cook in 176-185° F (80-85° C) water for 20 minutes. Place sausages in cold water for 5 minutes. Remove and let them cool.

Currywurst

Currywurst is the perfect sausage for vegetarians. Currywurst is all about the sauce and not the sausage so most vegetarian sausages qualify for making currywurst. Currywurst sausage is defined *not by the ingredients* which are inside of the sausage, but by the addition of *curry ketchup* during serving. This means that one can choose any sausage and as long as it is served with "curry flavored ketchup" it qualifies to be called Currywurst. As there are different types of curry and different types of the sauce produced, considerable variations occur between sausages.

Currywurst is the best selling sausage in Germany. Currywurst is to Germans what hot dog is to Americans. In New York hotdogs are sold with ketchup, mustard or sauerkraut on every street corner, in Berlin currywurst is served with "curry ketchup." Currywurst is consumed everywhere: in Berlin, Hamburg and the industrial Ruhr Area, it is sold by street cart vendors, small restaurants or served at home. Ready to use curry ketchups and sauces are sold in supermarkets. Currywurst is usually served with a roll, bread or french fries.

Photo 5.14 Currywurst in Berlin.

Photo 5.15 Currywurst in Berlin.

Photo 5.16 Currywurst.

Photo 5.17 Currywurst.

The simplest way to make currywurst sauce is to mix curry powder with tomato ketchup according to your own liking. Then sauce is poured over the sausage which is usually sliced into smaller pieces.

Photo 5.18 Homemade currywurst.

The demand for ready to use currywurst sauce in Germany is so great that Heinz Company makes ready to use Currywurst Flavored Ketchup and Knorr Company makes ready to mix with water powdered Currywurst Sauce. Those products can be obtained in the USA online as well.

Photo 5.19 Hela brand hot and mild currywurst sauce.

Photo 5.20 Currywurst sauce made by Knorr®.

Sausage: choose any sausage from this book, for example Basic, Chorizo, Bread Crumbs or Smoked Sausage.

Currywurst Sauce

Salt, 5.0 g (0.17 oz)
Curry powder, 30 g (1.05 oz)
Sugar, 20.0 g (0.70 oz)
Pepper, 4.0 g (0.14 oz)
Paprika, 4.0 g (0.14 oz)
Tomato sauce, 850 g (30 oz)
Onion powder, 10 g (0.35 oz)

Photo 5.21 Bread crumbs sausage with currywurst sauce.

Making Currywurst Sauce

Pour tomato sauce into a preheated skillet.
Add all ingredients and mix together.
Bring to a boil, reduce heat and simmer for 5 minutes.
Peel the casing off the sausage, then fry/broil/grill sausage on each side until brown and cooked.
Slice sausage into 1/2 inch thick pieces.
Pour curry sauce over hot sausage
Serve with bread roll or potato fries.

Notes

- Onion powder may be substituted with 1 medium size onion (60 g). Fry the onion in 2 table spoons (28 g) vegetable oil until glassy looking, then simmer with tomato sauce and other ingredients.

- Red vinegar may be added (1/4 cup, 60 ml).

- You can add some Latin flavor to the sausage by adding cilantro, garlic, lemon juice and some cayenne pepper.

History of Currywurst

The invention of currywurst is attributed to Herta Heuwer in Berlin in 1949 after she obtained ketchup, Worcestershire sauce and curry powder from British soldiers. She mixed these ingredients with other spices and poured it over grilled pork sausage. Heuwer started selling the cheap but filling snack at a street stand in the Charlottenburg district where it became popular with construction workers rebuilding the devastated city. She patented her sauce, called *Chillup*, in 1951. At its height the stand was selling 10,000 servings per week. She later opened a small restaurant which operated until 1974.

Due to the popularity of the sausage, in 2010 "Currywurst Museum" was opened in Berlin. The place attracts hundreds of visitors every day.

Currywurst Museum, Schützenstraße 70, 10117 Berlin, Germany.

www.currywurstmuseum.com

Photo 5.22 Currywurst museum in Berlin.

Erbswurst

Erbswurst is German sausage made from pea flour, pork belly, beef or pork fat, onions, salt and spices. Homemade Erbwurst sausage can be sliced and eaten as a snack or dissolved in hot water to make a nutritious and rich in calories pea soup. The product has almost unlimited shelf life, it is cheap to make and easy to prepare. The Erbwurst is a *survival food sausage and has been popular with hikers and expeditions.* It is somewhat related to Indian Pemmican as both products contain a large amount of fat and the manufacturing process is similar. The difference is that instead of pea flour the Pemmican uses powdered dry meat. Both products are perfect survival food.

Vegetarian Erbswurst

This is a vegetarian version of Erbswurst made without meat. Due to the large amount of pea flour soy emulsion containing 16% of oil is added, otherwise the sausage will feel very dry. This, by all means is not a large percentage as some fresh meat sausages are allowed to contain 50% of fat.

Erbswurst

Green pea flour, 300 g (0.66 lb)
Tofu, firm, 200 g (7 oz)
Soy emulsion (1:4:5)*, 400 g (0.88 lb)
Cracker meal, 50 g (1.76 oz)
Water for cracker meal,
100 ml (3.3 oz fl)
Red jalapenos, 50 g (1.76 oz)
Potato starch, 20 g (0.7 oz)
Guar gum, 10 g (0.3 oz)
Carrageenan, 10 g (0.35 oz)
Salt, 10 g (0.35 oz)
Pepper, 4 g (0.14 oz)
Garlic powder, 5 g (0.17 oz)
Vinegar, 50 ml (1.66 oz fl)

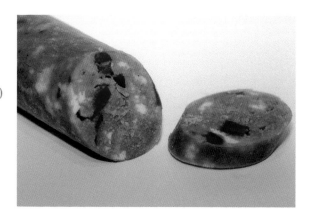

Photo 5.23 Erbswurst with tofu and jalapenos.

*Soy emulsion, 40 g soy protein isolate : 160 ml oil : 200 ml water. Blend protein with water first then gradually add oil.

Soak cracker meal in water.
Dice jalapenos and cut tofu into 1/8" (3 mm) cubes.
Mix pea flour with soy emulsion then add tofu, cracker meal, vinegar, jalapenos and spices.
Lastly, add starch, guar and carrageenan and mix everything again.
Stuff hard into 38 mm casings.
Cook in 176-185° F (80-85° C) water for 20 minutes. Place sausages in cold water for 5 minutes. Remove and let them cool.

History

The Erbwurst was invented in 1867 in Berlin by Johann Heinrich Grüneberg who was a cook and food canner. His invention was immediately purchased by the Prussian Army which introduced the product as the main mail for the soldier. When the war between France and Prussia broke out in 1870 the factories were producing thousands pounds of Erbswurst daily.

Since 1889 the Knorr company has been manufacturing Knorr Erbswurst and the sausage is still being sold in Germany. When Erbswurt is mixed with water an instant pea soup is created. It may be considered to be the first instant soup in history.

Photo 5.24 Knorr® Erbswurst is presliced.

Photo 5.25 Erbswurst soup.

Diluting a section of the sausage in hot water creates an instant pea soup. Erbswurst can be made from green or yellow pea flour.

Garam Masala

White rice, boiled, 600 g (1.32 lb)
Flaxseed emulsion (1:2:2), 100 g (3.5 oz)
Apple sauce, 100 g (3.5 oz)
Dry cranberries, 100 g (3.5 oz)
Sugar, 20 g (0.7 oz)
Potato starch, 15 g (0.52 oz)
Guar gum, 5 g (0.17 oz)
Carrageenan, 10 g (0.34 oz)
Cinnamon, 2 g (0.07 oz)
Garam masala spice, 10 g (0.34 oz)

Photo 5.26 Garam Masala Sausage.

Chop cranberries and mix with apple sauce. Mix rice with flaxseed emulsion, add apple sauce, sugar and spices. Add starch, guar, carrageenan and mix all together. Stuff hard into 38 mm casings. Cook in 176-185° F (80-85° C) water for 20 minutes. Place sausages in cold water for 5 minutes. Remove and let them cool.

Garbanzo Sausage

The chickpea is also known as gram or garbanzo bean. It is one of the earliest cultivated legumes.

Green pea flour, 300 g (0.66 lb)
Tofu, firm, 200 g (7 oz)
Soy emulsion (1:4:5)*, 400 g (0.88 lb)
TVP, 20 g (0.7 oz)
Cracker meal, 50 g (1.76 oz)
Water for cracker meal and TVP, 120 ml (4 oz fl)
Potato starch, 20 g (0.7 oz)
Guar gum, 10 g (0.3 oz)
Carrageenan, 10 g (0.35 oz)
Vinegar, 50 ml (1.66 oz fl)
Salt, 10 g (0.35 g)
Pepper, 4 g (0.14 oz)
Garlic powder, 5 g (0.17 oz)
Nutmeg, 0.5 g (0.01 oz)

Photo 5.27 Tofu pieces act as show material.

*Soy emulsion, 40 g soy protein isolate : 160 ml oil : 200 ml water. Blend protein with water first then gradually add oil.
Soak cracker meal and TVP in water.
Dice jalapenos and cut tofu into 1/8" (3 mm) cubes.
Mix pea flour with soy emulsion then add tofu, cracker meal, vinegar, jalapenos and spices.
Lastly, add starch, guar and carrageenan and mix everything again.
Stuff hard into 38 mm casings.
Cook in 176-185° F (80-85° C) water for 20 minutes. Place sausages in cold water for 5 minutes. Remove and let them cool.

Granola

Granola is a popular snack food, known as a "flapjack" in the United Kingdom, and as a "muesli bar" or "cereal bar" in Australia and New Zealand. It consists of rolled oats, nuts, honey, that is usually baked until crisp. Dried fruits, such as raisins and dates, are sometimes added. Honey is often substituted with golden syrup, brown sugar brings more flavor than white sugar. Granola is also often eaten by those who are hiking, camping, or backpacking because it is lightweight, high in calories, and easy to store. Granola that includes flax seeds is often used to improve digestion.

Cooked rolled oats, 600 g (1.32 lb)
Flaxseed emulsion (1:2:2), 200 g (7 oz)
Honey (or maple), 30 g (1.05 oz)
Brown sugar, 30 g (1.05 oz)
Dry raisins, 50 g (1.76 oz)
Dry cranberries, 50 g (1.76 oz)
Crushed pecans, 30 g (1.05 oz)
Starch, 25 g (0.88 oz)
Guar gum, 10 g (0.35 oz)
Carrageenan, 10 g (0.35 oz)
Cinnamon, 0.5 g (0.01 oz)
Vanilla extract, 15 ml (0.52 oz)

Photo 5.28a Granola Sausage.

Rolled oats are the plain instant type of oats. Oats to water ratio 1:2. Cook for 4 minutes.

Except starch, guar and carrageenan, mix all ingredients together. Add starch, guar and carrageenan and mix all together. Stuff hard into 38 mm casings.
Cook in 176-185° F (80-85° C) water for 20 minutes.
Place sausages in cold water for 5 minutes.
Remove and let them cool.

Photo 5.28b Granola Sausage.

Hot Dog

Ground wheat gluten, 750 g (1.65 lb)
Tofu, 100 g (3.5 oz)
SPI, 20 g (0.7 oz)
Potato flour, 30 (1.05 oz)
Oil, 30 ml (1 oz fl)
Potato starch, 30 (1.05 oz)
Guar gum, 10 g (0.35 oz)
Carrageenan, 10 g (0.35 oz)
Salt, 10 g (0.34 oz)
Pepper, 4 g (0.14 oz)
Coriander, 2 g (0.07 oz)
Paprika, 4 g (0.14 oz)
Annatto, 4 g (0.14 oz)
Nutmeg, 1 g (0.03 oz)
Allspice, 1 g (0.03 oz)
Onion powder, 5 g (0.17 oz)
Garlic powder, 5 g (0.17 oz)
Ginger, 0.5 g (0.01 g)
Cayenne, 0.5 g (0.01 g)

Photo 5.29 Hot Dog.

Mix oil with potato flour to make a paste. Except the oil paste, starch, guar and carrageenan, blend all other ingredients together. You might need some water - apply as little as possible. Lastly, add oil paste, flour, starch, guar, carrageenan and mix all together. Stuff hard into 38 mm casings. Cook in 176-185° F (80-85° C) water for 20 minutes. Place sausages in cold water for 5 minutes. Remove and let them cool.

Hunter Sausage

Photo 5.30 Hunter Sausage.

Ground wheat gluten, 500 g (1.10 lb)
Cooked rice, 200 g (7.0 oz)
Flaxseed emulsion (1:2:2), 100 g (3.5 oz)
Potato starch, 20 g (0.7 oz)
Guar gum, 5 g (0.17 oz)
Carrageenan, 10 g (0.35 oz)
Potato flour, 40 g (1.41 oz)
Onion, 50 g (1.76 oz)
Mushrooms, 50 g (1.76 oz)
Oil, 30 ml (1 oz fl)
Potato flour (for onions), 10 g (0.35 oz)
Salt, 10 g (0.35 oz)
Pepper, 4 g (0.14 oz)
Marjoram, 2 g (0.07 oz)
Coriander, 2 g (0.07 oz)
Chopped parsley, 3 Tbsp

Finely chop onion and mushrooms. Fry on medium heat in a little oil until onions are glassy and light yellow. Stir in potato flour and cook 4 minutes longer. Let cool. Except potato flour, starch, guar and carrageenan, mix all ingredients. Add starch, guar and carrageenan and mix again. Lastly, add potato flour and mix all again. Stuff hard into 38 mm casings. Cook in 176-185° F (80-85° C) water for 20 minutes. Place sausages in cold water for 5 minutes. Remove and let them cool.

Italian Sausage

Ground wheat gluten, 850 g, (1.87 lb)
SPC 20 g, (0.7 oz)
Oil 40 ml (1.3 oz fl)
Vital wheat gluten flour, 80 g (2.82 oz)
Carrageenan, 10 g (0.35 oz)
Guar gum, 5 g (0.17 oz)
Salt, 12 g (0.42 oz)
Cayenne, 1.0 g (0.03 oz)
Fennel seed, cracked, 4.0 g (0.14 oz)
Coriander, 1.0 g (0.03 oz)
Caraway, 1.0 g (0.03 oz)

Photo 5.31 Italian Sausage.

Mix oil with soy protein concentrate to create a paste. Mix all ingredients except gluten flour, carrageenan and guar. Lastly add gluten flour, carrageenan and guar and mix all together. Stuff hard into 38 mm casings.
Cook in 176-185° F (80-85° C) water for 20 minutes. Place sausages in cold water for 5 minutes. Remove and let them cool.

Lentil Sausage

Lentils have been one of the first crops cultivated by humans. Lentil colors range from yellow to red-orange to green, brown and black. Lentils also vary in size and are sold in many forms, with or without the skins, whole or split.

Cooked lentils, 600 g (1.32 lb)
Flaxseed emulsion (1:2:2), 200 g (7 oz)
Tofu, 100 g (3.5 oz)
Starch, 25 g (0.88 oz)
Guar, 10 g (0.35 oz)
Carrageenan, 10 g (0.35 oz)
Potato flour, 50 g (1.76 oz)
Salt, 12 g (0.42 oz)
Pepper, 4 g (0.14 oz)
Cumin, 4 g (0.14 oz)
Vinegar, 15 ml (0.5 oz fl)

Photo 5.32 Lentil Sausage.

Bring water to a boil, add lentils and simmer for 25 minutes. Drain.
Mix lentils, emulsion, tofu, vinegar and spices together.
Add starch, guar, carrageenan and mix again. Add potato flour and mix all together. Stuff hard into 38 mm casings.
Cook in 176-185° F (80-85° C) water for 20 minutes. Place sausages in cold water for 5 minutes. Remove and let them cool.

Oats Sausage

Oats come as rolled (instant type), steel cut or whole grain. Steel cut oats provide the best texture and feel.

Boiled steel cut oats, 750 g (1.65 lb)
Flaxseed emulsion (1:2:2), 100 g (3.5 oz)
Raisins, 60 g (2.11 oz)
Potato flour, 50 g (1.76 oz)
Potato starch, 20 g (0.7 oz)
Guar gum, 10 g (0.35 oz)
Carrageenan, 10 g (0.35 oz)
Sugar, 50 g (1.76 oz)
Cinnamon, 2 g (0.07 oz)

Photo 5.33a Oats Sausage.

Use 1 part of steel cut oats to 3 parts of water. Bring water to a boil, add oats and boil at low heat for 15 minutes. Switch off the heat, remove the lid and let the oats to cool.
Soak raisins in water for 30 minutes and then drain.
Mix all ingredients together.
Stuff hard into 38 mm casings.
Cook in 176-185° F (80-85° C) water for 20 minutes. Place sausages in cold water for 5 minutes. Remove and let them cool.

Photo 5.33b Oats Sausage.

Peanut Butter

Cooked steel cut oats, 350 g (0.77 lb)
Flaxseed coconut emulsion
(1:4), 300 g (0.66 lb)
Creamy peanut butter, 200 g (7 oz)
Cocoa baking powder, 30 g (1.05 oz)
Honey (maple syrup), 30 g (1.05 oz)
Sugar, 30 g (1.05 oz)
Raisins, 50 g (1.76 oz)
Starch, 25 g (0.88 oz)
Guar gum, 10 g (0.35 oz)
Carrageenan, 10 g (0.35 oz)
Cinnamon, 0.5 g (0.01 oz)

Photo 5.34 Peanut Butter Sausage.

Cook 1 part of oats in 3 parts of water.
Soak raisins for 30 minutes in water. Drain.
Make emulsion blending 60 g of ground flaxseed with 240 ml (8 oz fl) of coconut milk. Add cocoa powder and mix again. Mix emulsion with oats, peanut butter, honey, sugar, raisins and spices. Add starch, guar and carrageenan and mix all together.
Stuff hard into 38 mm casings. Cook in 176-185° F (80-85° C) water for 20 minutes. Place sausages in cold water for 5 minutes. Remove and let them cool.

Polenta with Cranberries

Polenta is cornmeal boiled into a porridge. Polenta has a creamy texture due to the gelatinization of starch in the grain. Polenta takes 35-45 minutes to cook, typically simmering in water in four times its volume with almost constant stirring, necessary for even gelatinization of the starch.

Polenta, 750 g (1.65 lb)
Cranberries, 50 g (1.76 oz)
Raisins, 50 g (1.76 oz)
Sugar, 25 g (0.88 oz)
Maple syrup, 30 ml (1 oz fl)
Vanilla extract, 30 ml (1 oz fl)
Potato starch, 25 g (0.88 oz)
Guar gum, 15 g (0.53 oz)
Carrageenan, 10 g (0.35 oz)

Photo 5.35 Polenta with Cranberries Sausage.

Mix 1 cup of cornmeal with 2 parts of *cold* water. In a separate pot bring 1-1/2 cup of water to a boil. Add soaked cornmeal and simmer for 35 minutes stirring often.

Add maple syrup, vanilla, chopped unsoaked cranberries and raisins to 750 g of cool polenta. Stir together. Add starch, guar gum and carrageenan and mix. Stuff hard into 38 mm casings. Cook in 176-185° F (80-85° C) water for 20 minutes. Place sausages in cold water for 5 minutes. Remove and let them cool.

Poppy Seed

This recipe is based on Kutia - sweet, grain and poppy seed pudding, traditionally served at Christmas in Ukraine, Belarus, Russian and Eastern parts of Poland. It is usually made with whole grain wheat, although some versions incorporate buckwheat or barley groats. Other ingredients are poppy seed, nuts, raisins and honey.

Photo 5.36a Poppy Seed Sausage.

The tiny poppy seeds are used, whole or ground, as an ingredient in many foods, and they are pressed to yield poppy seed oil. Fillings in pastries are sometimes made of finely ground poppy seeds mixed with butter or milk and sugar. The filling may be flavored with lemon or orange zest, rum and vanilla with raisins, heavy cream, cinnamon, and chopped blanched almonds or walnuts added. Bagels are often sprinkled with poppy seeds.

Whole wheat grain, 600 g (1.32 lb)
Poppy seed (drained weight)*, 200 g (7 oz)
Sugar, 60 g (2.11 oz)
Honey (maple syrup), 30 g (1.05 oz)
Potato starch, 20 g (0.7 oz)
Guar gum, 10 g (0.35 oz)
Carrageenan, 10 g (0.35 oz)
Crushed pecans, 50 g (1.76 oz)
Raisins (dry weight), 50 g (1.76 oz)
Vanilla, 15 ml (0.5 oz fl)
Water as needed, 100-200 ml (3.3-6.6 oz fl)

Photo 5.36b Poppy Seed Sausage.

Use 1 cup of wheat to 2-1/2 cups of water. Bring water to a boil, add wheat, cover and simmer on low heat for about 1 hour until tender. If the water is absorbed before the grains are tender, add more as needed. Stir from time to time. Drain the grains. Return the grains to the hot pot, let them steam for 10 minutes uncovered.
Bring water to a boil, switch the heat off. Add poppy seed, stir and leave for 5 minutes. This removes some of poppy seed bitterness. Drain*.
Soak raisins in water for 30 minutes. Drain.
Using mixing bowl combine wheat, poppy seeds, sugar, walnuts, raisins, vanilla and water together.
Add starch, guar and carrageenan and mix all together. Stuff hard into 38 mm casings. Cook in 176-185° F (80-85° C) water for 20 minutes. Place sausages in cold water for 5 minutes. Remove and let them cool.

Potato Sausage

Boiled potatoes, 500 g (0.88 lb)
Tofu, 100 g (3.5 oz)
Textured vegetable protein, 100 g (3.5 oz)
(water for TVP), 220 ml (7.3 oz fl)
Potato flour, 50 g (1.76 oz)
Potato starch, 20 g (0.7 oz)
Guar gum, 10 g (0.35 oz)
Carrageenan, 10 g (0.35 oz)
Salt, 12 g (0.42 oz)
White pepper, 4 g (0.14 oz)
Allspice, ground, 2 g (0.07 oz)
Onion powder, 10 g (0.35 oz)
Salt, 12 g (0.42 oz)
White pepper, 4 g (0.14 oz)
Allspice, ground, 2 g (0.07 oz)
Onion powder, 10 g (0.35 oz)
Cinnamon, 0.5 g (0.01 oz)
Dry parsley flakes, 1 Tbsp
Water as needed, 100 ml (3.3 oz)

Photo 5.37 Potato Sausage.

Soak TVP in 220 ml of water for 20 minutes. Mix with potatoes, tofu and all spices (except flour, starch, guar and carrageenan). Add starch, guar, carrageenan, flour and around 100 ml water and mix all together. Stuff hard into 38 mm casings. Cook in 176-185° F (80-85° C) water for 20 minutes. Place sausages in cold water for 5 minutes. Remove and let them cool.

Quinoa with Black Beans

Quinoa grain originated in the Andean region of Bolivia, Peru, Ecuador, Chile and Colombia, where it was consumed already 3,000 to 4,000 years ago. The seeds are cooked the same way as rice and can be used in a wide range of dishes. Quinoa is classified as a source of a complete protein that contains an adequate proportion of all nine of the essential amino acids necessary for the dietary needs of humans.

Photo 5.38 Quinoa with Black Beans.

Cooked quinoa, 500 g (1.10 lb)
Black beans, 300 g (10.5 oz)
Flaxseed emulsion (1:2:2), 100 g (3.5 oz)
Potato starch, 25 g (0.88 oz)
Guar gum, 5 g (0.17 oz)
Carrageenan, 10 g (0.35 oz)
Curry spice, 10 g (0.35 oz)

The following ingredients go well with quinoa - lemon juice, chile peppers, oregano, cilantro, tomatoes, red bell pepper.

Cook quinoa like rice, use 1 cup quinoa : 2 cups water.
Mix quinoa, beans, emulsion and spices.
Add starch, guar, carrageenan and mix all together.
Stuff hard into 38 mm casings.
Cook in 176-185° F (80-85° C) water for 20 minutes. Place sausages in cold water for 5 minutes. Remove and let them cool.

Rice Sausage with Apple Sauce

Rice, boiled, 650 g (1.54 lb)
Apple sauce, 200 g (7 oz)
Vital wheat gluten flour, 80 g (2.82 oz)
Soy protein isolate, 20 g (0.7 oz)
Sugar, 30 g (1.05 oz)
Raisins (dry), 50 g (1.76 oz)
Potato starch, 10 g (0.35 oz)
Guar gum, 5 g (0.17 oz)
Carrageenan, 10 g (0.35 oz)
Cinnamon, 2 g (0.07 oz)
Ground cloves, 0.25 g 1 clove
Vanilla extract, 5 ml (1 tsp)
Water as needed, 100 ml (3.3 oz fl)

Photo 5.39 Rice with Apple Sauce sausage.

Mix apple sauce with raisins, vanilla extract and spices. Add rice, sugar, soy protein isolate and mix. Add starch, guar, carrageenan and mix. Add vital wheat flour and mix all together. Add water as necessary.
Stuff hard into 38 mm casings. Cook in 176-185° F (80-85° C) water for 20 minutes.
Place sausages in cold water for 5 minutes. Remove and let them cool.

Sausage with Cranberries

Ground wheat gluten, 700 g (1.54 lb)
Soy protein emulsion, 100 g (3.5 oz)
Vital wheat gluten flour, 60 g (2.11 oz)
Potato starch, 20 g (0.7 oz)
Guar gum, 10 g (0.35 oz)
Carrageenan, 10 g (0.35 oz)
Dry cranberries, 50 g
Salt, 5 g (0.17 oz)
Sugar, 10 g (0.35 oz)
Allspice, 1 g (0.01 oz)
Onion powder, 10 g (0.35 oz)
Cinnamon, 0.3 g (0.01 oz)

Photo 5.40 Sausage with Cranberries.

Grind wheat gluten through a small plate. Chop cranberries and soak for 30 minutes in water. Drain.
Mix all ingredients except vital wheat gluten flour, starch, guar and carrageenan.
Add vital wheat gluten flour, starch, guar and carrageenan and mix all together.
Stuff hard into 38 mm casings. Cook in 176-185° F (80-85° C) water for 20 minutes.
Place sausages in cold water for 5 minutes. Remove and let them cool.

Smoked Sausage

Wheat gluten, 800 g (1.76 lb)
Soy emulsion, 100 g (3.5 oz)
Vital wheat gluten, 50 g (1.76 oz)
Potato starch, 20 g (0.7 oz)
Guar gum, 10 g (0.35 oz)
Carrageenan, 10 g (0.35 oz)
Salt, 10 g (0.35 oz)
Pepper, 4 g (0.14 oz)
Marjoram, 1 g (0.03 oz)
Garlic powder, 5 g (0.17 oz)
Liquid smoke, 15 ml (0.5 oz fl)

Photo 5.41 Smoked Sausage.

Grind wheat gluten through 3/8" (10 mm) plate.
Mix ground gluten with emulsion and spices. Add vital wheat gluten, starch, guar, carrageenan and carrageenan and mix all together.
Stuff hard into 38 mm casings. Cook in 176-185° F (80-85° C) water for 20 minutes.
Place sausages in cold water for 5 minutes. Remove and let them cool.

Teff Snack Sausage

This tiny size, in fact, makes teff ideally suited to semi-nomadic life in areas of Ethiopia and Eritrea where it has long thrived. Since teff's bran and germ make up a large percentage of the tiny grain and it's too small to process, teff is always eaten in its whole form.

Cooked teff, 500 g (1.10 lb)
Creamy peanut butter, 150 g (5.29 oz)
Flaxseed emulsion (1:2:2), 150 g (5.29 oz)
Dry raisins, 50 g (1.76 oz)
Crushed pecans, 50 g (1.76 oz)
Brown sugar, 30 g (1.05 oz)
Honey (maple), 30 g (1.05 oz)
Potato starch, 20 g (0.7 oz)
Guar gum, 10 g (0.35 oz)
Carrageenan, 10 g (0.35 oz)
Vanilla extract, 15 ml (0.5 oz fl)

Soak raisins in water for 30 minutes. Drain.

Photo 5.42 Teff Snack Sausage.

Use 1 cup teff : 1 cup water. Bring the water to a boil. Gradually stir in teff, reduce heat, add a pinch of salt, cover and cook for 6 minutes, stirring often until the water is absorbed.

Mix teff, peanut butter, emulsion, raisins, pecans, sugar, honey and vanilla extract together. Add starch, guar, carrageenan and mix all together.
Stuff hard into 38 mm casings. Cook in 176-185° F (80-85° C) water for 20 minutes.
Place sausages in cold water for 5 minutes. Remove and let them cool.

Tofu Sausage with Nori

Tofu, 400 g (0.88 lb)
Soaked Nori, 250 g (0.55 lb)
Bread crumbs, 200 g (7 oz)
Potato flour, 50 g (1.76 lb)
Starch, 25 g (0.88 oz)
Guar gum, 10 g (0.35 oz)
Carrageenan, 10 g (0.35 oz)
Salt, 10 g (0.35 oz)
Pepper, 5 g (0.17 oz)
Onion powder, 5 g (0.17 oz)
Ginger, 0.5 g (0.01 oz)
Soy sauce, 15 ml (0.5 oz fl)

Photo 5.43 Tofu with Nori Sausage.

Soak about 100 g (3.5 oz) of crushed Nori seaweed (see page 42) in 500 ml (2 cups) of water for 60 minutes. Drain. Measure 250 g. Grind or mash tofu and mix seaweeds, bread crumbs, soy sauce and spices. Add starch, guar and carrageenan and mix. Add potato flour and mix all together. Stuff hard into 38 mm casings. Cook in 176-185° F (80-85° C) water for 20 minutes. Place sausages in cold water for 5 minutes. Remove and let them cool.

Tomato Sausage with Diced Tomatoes

Diced tomatoes, 300 g, (10.58 oz)
Textured vegetable protein, 100 g (3.5 oz)
Tofu, 100 g (2.5 oz)
Cracker meal, 200 g
Tomato paste, 30 g (1.05 oz)
Water for cracker meal, 200 ml (6.6 oz)
Potato starch, 20 g (0.7 oz)
Guar gum, 10 g (0.35 oz)
Carrageenan, 10 g (0.35 oz)
Salt, 10 g (0.35 oz)
Pepper, 2.0 g (0.07 oz)
Garlic powder, 5 g (0.17 oz)
Basil, 2 g (0.07 oz)
Thyme, 2 g (0.07 oz)
Oregano, 2 g (0.07 oz)
Onion, 10 g (0.35 oz)
Maggi® seasoning, 5 ml (1 tsp)
Add water if needed, 100 ml (3.3 oz fl)

Photo 5.44 Diced Tomato Sausage.

1. Soak cracker meal in 200 ml of water. Mix dry TVP, diced tofu, diced tomatoes and cracker meal together. Add more water if necessary. Cracker meal is a coarse flour which is made from finely milled crackers. It is often used as a seafood fry mix. It can be replaced with bread crumbs.

2. Except starch, guar and carrageenan, add all spices and mix. Add tomato paste, starch, guar, carrageenan and mix all together. Stuff hard into 38 mm casings. Cook in water at 176-185° F (80-85° F) for 20 minutes. Remove and place for 5 minutes in cold water. Remove from water and let it cool.

Tomato Sausage with Tomato Sauce

Tomato Sauce, 600 ml (20 oz fl)
TVP, 80 g, (2.82 oz)
Tofu, 100 g (3.5 oz)
Tomato paste, 30 g (1.05 oz)
Cracker meal, 200 g (7 oz)
Potato starch, 20 g (0.7 oz)
Guar gum, 10 g (0.35 oz)
Carrageenan, 10 g (0.35 oz)
Salt, 10 g (0.35 oz)
Pepper, 2.0 g (0.07 oz)
Garlic powder, 5 g (0.17 oz)
Basil, 2 g (0.07 oz)
Thyme, 2 g (0.07 oz)
Oregano, 2 g (0.07 oz)
Onion, 10 g (0.35 oz)
Maggi® seasoning, 5 ml (1 tsp)

Photo 5.45 Tomato Sauce Sausage.

Mix dry TVP, diced tofu, cracker meal, tomato sauce and paste together. Except starch, guar and carrageenan, add all spices and mix. Add starch, guar, carrageenan and mix all together. Stuff hard into 38 mm casings. Cook in water at 176-185° F (80-85° F) for 20 minutes. Remove and place for 5 minutes in cold water. Remove from water and let it cool.

White Tofu Sausage

Tofu, 450 g (0.99 lb)
Cooked steel cut oats, 400 g (0.88 lb)
Soy emulsion (1:4:5), 50 g (1.76 oz)
Potato flour, 50 g (1.76 oz)
Starch, 20 g (0.7 oz)
Guar gum, 10 g (0.35 oz)
Carrageenan, 10 g (0.35 oz)
Salt, 10 g (0.35 oz)
Pepper, 4 g (0.14 oz)
Nutmeg, 1 g (0.03 oz)
Cloves, ground, 0.5 g (1 clove)

Bring 1.2 liter of water to a boil.
Add 400 g steel cut oats and simmer
for 30 minutes. Let cool.

Photo 5.46 Tofu Sausage.

Mix diced tofu, oats, emulsion and spices together. Add starch, guar and carrageenan and mix. Add flour and mix all together.
Stuff hard into 38 mm casings. Cook in water at 176-185° F (80-85° F) for 20 minutes. Remove and place for 5 minutes in cold water. Remove from water and let it cool.

Links of Interest

Sausage Making Equipment and Supplies

The Sausage Maker Inc., Equipment, casings, proteins, flours, spices, gums
1500 Clinton St., Building 123
Buffalo, NY 14206, 888-490-8525; 716-824-5814
www.sausagemaker.com

Flours - Grains - Seeds - Gums

Amazon, A great variety of equipment and supplies
www.amazon.con

Barry Farm Foods, Flours and other ingredients
www.barryfarm.com

Bob's Red Mill, Grains, flours, starches, molecular gastronomy
www.bobsredmill.com

Bulk Foods, Grains, flours, starches, dried fruits, molecular gastronomy
www.bulkfoods.com

Konjac Foods, Konjac gum
www.konjacfoods.com

Lepicerie, Gums, baking supplies
www.lepicerie.com

Modernist Pantry, Cooking supplies

www.modernistpantry.com

Moutain Rose Herbs, Herbs, spices, essential oils, gums
www.mountainroseherbs.com

Pacific Pectin, Pectins, LM pectin
www.pacificpectin.com

Will Powder Molecular gastronomy-gums
www.willpowder.net

USDA Nutrient Database
www.nal.usda.gov/fnic/foodcomp/search

FITDAY™
www.fitday.com

Calorie Control Council
www.caloriecontrol.org

Dietary Guidelines for Americans
www.health.gov/dietaryguidelines/dga2005/document

USDA Agricultural Research Service
www.ars.usda.gov/main/main.htm

Whole Grains Council
wholegrainscouncil.org

FAO List of Roots and Tubers
www.fao.org/es/faodef/fdef02e.htm

Meats and Sausages, All about sausage making
www.meatsandsausages.com

Index

More Books by Stanley and Adam Marianski

More information can be found at www.bookmagic.com

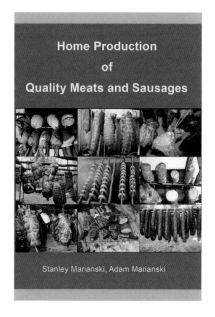

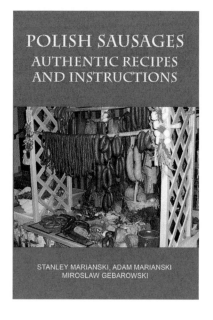

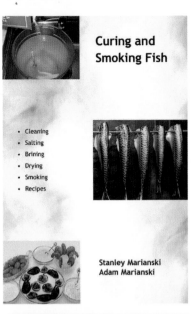

Curing and Smoking Fish

- Cleaning
- Salting
- Brining
- Drying
- Smoking
- Recipes

Stanley Marianski
Adam Marianski

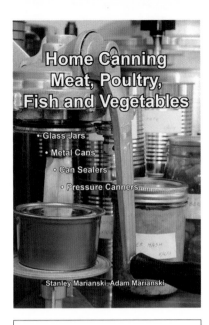

Home Canning Meat, Poultry, Fish and Vegetables

- Glass Jars
- Metal Cans
- Can Sealers
- Pressure Canners

Stanley Marianski, Adam Marianski

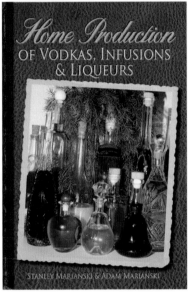

Home Production of Vodkas, Infusions & Liqueurs

STANLEY MARIANSKI & ADAM MARIANSKI

MAKING HEALTHY SAUSAGES

- Reduced Fat
- Low Salt
- Extended Value
- Kosher
- Vegetarian

Stanley and Adam Marianski

THE AMAZING MULLET

HOW TO CATCH, SMOKE AND COOK THE FISH

ADAM MARIANSKI

SAUERKRAUT, KIMCHI, PICKLES & RELISHES

Stanley Marianski, Adam Marianski

Printed in Great Britain
by Amazon